DECENTRALISM

Decentralism
where it came from
where is it going?

mildred j. loomis

BLACK
ROSE
BOOKS

Montreal/New York/London

Black Rose Books No. II331

National Library of Canada Cataloguing in Publication Data

Loomis, Mildred J.

Decentralism : where it came from--where is it going? / Mildred J. Loomis

Includes bibliographical references and index.

ISBN: 1-55164-249-2 (bound)   ISBN: 1-55164-248-4 (pbk.)

(alternative ISBNs 9781551642499 [bound]   9781551642482 [pbk.])

1. Decentralization in government--United States. 2. Communitarianism--
United States--History. 3. Cooperation--United States--History.
4. Green movement--United States--History. I. Title.

HT123.L655 2004   307   C2004-905038-9

Our thanks to the School of Living (www.s-o-l.org) for permission to reprint this work.

Cover design: Associés libres

BLACK ROSE BOOKS

C.P. 1258	2250 Military Road	99 Wallis Road
Succ. Place du Parc	Tonawanda, NY	London, E9 5LN
Montréal, H2X 4A7	14150	England
Canada	USA	UK

To order books:
In Canada: (phone) 1-800-565-9523 (fax) 1-800-221-9985

email: utpbooks@utpress.utoronto.ca
In United States: (phone) 1-800-283-3572 (fax) 1-651-917-6406
In the UK & Europe: (phone) London 44 (0)20 8986-4854
(fax) 44 (0)20 8533-5821

email: order@centralbooks.com
Our Web Site address: http://www.web.net/blackrosebooks
A publication of the Institute of Policy Alternatives of Montréal (IPAM)
Printed in Canada

contents

foreword
Reflections on Decentralism[1]
By george woodcock

I was asked to write on decentralism in history, and I find myself looking into shadows where small lights shine as fireflies do, endure a little, vanish, and then reappear like Auden's messages of the just. The history of decentralism has to be written largely in negative, in winters and twilights as well as springs and dawns, for it is a history which, like that of libertarian beliefs in general, is not observed in progressive terms. It is not the history of a movement, an evolution. It is the history of something that, like grass, has been with us from the human beginning, something that may go to earth, like bulbs in winter, and yet be there always, in the dark soil of human society, to break forth in unexpected places and at undisciplined times.

Palaeolithic man, food-gatherer and hunter, was a decentralist by necessity, because the earth did not provide enough wild food to allow crowding, and in modern remotenesses that were too wild or unproductive for civilized people to penetrate, humans still lived until very recently in primitive decentralism: Australian aborigines, Papuan inland villagers, Eskimos in northern Canada. Such people developed, before history touched them, their own complex techniques and cultures to defend a primitive and precarious way of life; they often developed remarkable artistic traditions as well, such as those of the Indians of the Pacific rain forests and some groups of Eskimos. But, since their world was one where concentration meant scarcity and death, they did not develop a political life that allowed the formation of authoritarian structures nor did they make an institution out of war. They practised mutual aid for survival, but this did not make them angels; they practised infanticide and the abandonment of elders for the same reason.

I think with feeling of those recently living decentralist societies because I have just returned from the Canadian Arctic where the last phase of traditional Eskimo life began as recently as a decade ago. Now, the old nomadic society, in which people moved about in extended families rather than tribes, is at an end, with all its skills abandoned, its traditions, songs and dances fading in the memory. Last year the cariboo-hunting Eskimos probably built their last igloo; now they are herded together into communities ruled by white men, where they live in groups of four to six hundred people, in imitation of white men's houses and with guaranteed welfare handouts when they cannot earn money by summer construction work. Their children are being taught by people who know no Eskimo, their young men are losing the skills of the hunt; power élites are beginning to appear in their crowded little northern slums, among a people who never knew what power meant, and the diminishing dog teams (now less than one family in four owns dogs and only about one family in twenty goes on extended hunting or trapping journeys) are symbolic of the loss of freedom among a people who have become physically and mentally dependent on the centralized, bureaucratic-ridden world which the Canadian Government has built it since it set out a few years ago to rescue the people of the North from "barbarism" and insecurity.

The fate of the Eskimos, and that of many primitive cultures during the past quarter of a century, shows that the old, primal decentralism of Stone Age mankind is doomed even when it has survived into the modern world. From now on, mankind will be decentralist by intent and experience, because he/she has known the evils of centralization and rejected them.

Centralization began when people settled on the land and cultivated it. Farmers joined together to protect their herds and field from other humans who still remained nomadic wanderers; to conserve and share out the precious waters; to placate the deities who held the gifts of fertility, the priest who served the deities, and the kings who later usurped the roles of priest and god alike. The little realms of local priest-kings grew into the great valley empires of Egypt and Mesopotamia, and over-towering these emerged the first attempt at a world empire, that of the Achaemenian Kings of Persia who established an administrative colossus which was the prototype of the centralized state, imitated by the despots of Northern India, the Hellenistic god-kings, and the divine Caesars of Rome.

We have little knowledge how mankind clung to their local loyalties and personal lives, how simple people tried to keep control of the affairs and things that concerned them most, in that age when writing recorded the deeds of kings and priests and had little to say about common men. But if we can judge from the highly traditional and at least partly autonomous village societies which still existed in India when the Moghuls arrived, and which had probably survived the centuries of political chaos and strife that lay between Moghuls and Guptas, it seems likely that the farther people in those ages lived away from the centres of power, the more they established and defended rights to use the land and govern their own local affairs, so long as the lord's tribute was paid. It was, after all, on the village communities that had survived through native and Moghul and British empires that Gandhi based his hopes of *panchayat raj*, a society based on autonomous peasant communes.

In Europe the Dark Ages after the Roman Empire were regarded by Victorian historians as a historical waste land ravaged by barbarian hordes and baronial bandits. But these ages were also in fact an interlude during which, in the absence of powerful centralized authorities, the decentralist urge appeared again, and village communes established forms of autonomy which in remoter areas, like the Pyrenees, the Alps and the Appennines, have survived into the present. To the same "Dark" Ages belong the earliest free city republics of mediaeval Europe, which arose at first for mutual protection in the ages of disorder, and which in Italy and Germany remained for centuries the homes of European learning and art and of such freedom as existed in the world of their time.

Out of such village communes and such cities arose, in Switzerland, the world's first political federation, based on the shared protection of local freedoms against feudal monarchs and renaissance despots.

DECENTRALISM

Some of these ancient communes exist to this day; the Swiss Canton of Appenzell still acts as a direct democracy in which every citizen takes part in the annual voting on laws; the Italian city state of San Marino still retains its mountain independence in a world of great states. But these are rare survivals, due mainly to geographic inaccessibility in days before modern transport.

As national states began to form at the end of the Middle Ages, the attack on decentralism was led not merely by the monarchs and dictators who established highly organized states like Bourbon France and Cromwellian England, but also by the Church and particularly by the larger monastic orders who in their house established rules of uniform behaviour and rigid timekeeping that anticipated the next great assault on local and independent freedom and on the practice of mutual aid; this happened when the villages of Britain and later of other European countries were depopulated in the Agricultural Revolution of the eighteenth century, and their homeless people drifted into the disciplined factories and suffered the alienation produced by the new industrial towns, where all traditional bonds were broken, and all the participation in common works that belonged to the mediaeval villages became irrelevant.

It was these developments, the establishment of the centralized state in the seventeenth century and of industrial centralization in the eighteenth and nineteenth centuries, that made mankind for the first time consciously aware of the necessity of decentralism to save them from the soulless world that was developing around them.

Against Cromwell's military state, Gerrard Winstanley and the original Diggers opposed their idea and practice of establishing new communes of landworkers on the waste lands of England, communes which would renounce overlords and extended participation and equality to men, women, and even children.

When the French Revolution took the way of centralism, establishing a more rigidly bureaucratic state than the Bourbons and introducing universal conscription for the first time, men like Jacques Roux and his fellows enragés protested in the name of the local communes of Paris, which they regarded as the bases of democratic organization, and at the same time in England William Godwin, the first of the philosophic anarchists, recognized the perils of forms of government which left decision making in the hands of men gathered at the top and centre of society. In his *Political Justice* Godwin envisaged countries in which assemblies of delegates would meet—seldom—to discuss matters of urgent common concern, in which no permanent organs of central government would be allowed to continue, and in which each local parish would decide its own affairs by free agreement (and not by majority vote) and matters of dispute would be settled by *ad hoc* juries of arbitration.

The British and French Utopian socialists of the early nineteenth century, as distinct from the Marxists and the revolutionary socialists led by Auguste Blanqui, were inspired by their revulsion against monolithic industrial and political organization to base the realization of their theories on small communal units which they believed could be established even before the existing society had been destroyed. At that period the American frontier lay still in the valley of the Mississippi, and there was a tendency—which existed until the end of the pioneering days—for the small pioneers societies of trappers and traders, miners and farmers, to organize themselves in largely autonomous communities, that managed their own affairs and in many senses of the word took the law into their own hands.

In this society, where people responded to frontier conditions by *ad hoc* participatory and decentralist organization, the European and American Utopian socialists, as well as various groups of Christian communities, tried to set up self-governing communes which would be the cells of the new fraternal world. The followers of Cabet and Fourier, of Robert Owen and Josiah Warren, all played their part in a movement which produced hundreds of communities and lasted almost a century; its last wave ebbed on the Pacific coast in the Edwardian era, when a large Finnish socialist community was established on the remote island of Sointula off the coast of British Columbia.

Only the religious communities of this era, which had a purpose outside mere social theory, survived; even today some of the Mennonite communities of Canada keep so closely to their ideals of communitarian autonomy that they are leaving the country to find in South America a region where they can be free to educate their children as they wish. The secular communities all vanished; the main lesson their failure taught was that decentralist organization must reach down to the roots of the present, to the needs of the actual human beings who participate, and not upward into the collapsing dream structures of a Utopian future.

Other great crises in the human situation have followed the industrial revolution, and every one has produced its decentralist movements in which men and women have turned away from the nightmares of megapolitics to the radical realities of human relationships. The crisis of the Indian struggle for independence caused Gandhi to preach the need to build society upon the foundation of the village. The bitter repressions of Tsarist Russia led Peter Kropotkin to develop his theories of a decentralised society integrating industry and agriculture, manual and mental skills. World War II led to considerable community movement among both British and American pacifists, seeking to create cells of sane living in the interstices of a belligerent world, and an even larger movement of decentralization and communitarianism has arisen in North America in contradiction to the society that can wage a war like that in Vietnam. Today it is likely that more people than ever before are consciously engaged in some kind of decentralist venture which expresses not merely rebellion against monolithic authoritarianism, but also faith in the possibility of a new, cellular kind of society in which at every level the participation in decision-making envisaged by nineteenth-century anarchists like Proudhon and Kropotkin will be developed.

As the monstrous and fatal flaws of modern economic and political centralism become more evident, as the State is revealed ever more convincingly as the enemy of all human love, the advocacy and practice of decentralism will spread more widely, if only because the necessity for it will become constantly more urgent. The less decentralist action is tied to rigid social and political theories, and especially to antediluvian ones like those of the Marxists, the more penetrating and durable its effects will be. The soils most favourable to the spread of decentralism are probably countries like India, where rural living still predominates, countries like Japan where the decentralization of factories and the integration of agricultural and industrial economies has already been recognized as a necessity for survival, and the places in our western world where the social rot has run deepest and the decentralists can penetrate like white ants. The moribund centres of the cities; the decaying marginal farmlands; these are the places which centralist governments using bankers' criteria of efficiency cannot possibly revivify, because the profit would not be financial but human. In such areas the small and flexible cell of workers, serving the needs of local people, can survive and continue simultaneously the tasks of quiet destruction and cellular building. But not all the work can be done in the shadows. There will still be the need for theoreticians to carry on the work which Kropotkin and Geddes and Mumford began in the past, of demonstrating the ultimately self-destructive character of political and industrial centralism, and showing how society as a whole, and not merely the lost corners of it, can be brought back to health and peace by breaking down the pyramids of authority, so that men can be given to eat the bread of brotherly love, and not the stones of power—of any power.

Note

1. Originally published in *Anarchy*, October 1969

pReface
By hazel henderson

This fascinating report of decentralist thought and action provides indispensable grounding for today's futurists and New Age activists in America. It is an important clarification of the philosophies of anarchism and mutual aid, and their roots in private property. We are shown how the perversion of private property rights for the *individual* led to the monstrous inequities that allowed multi-national corporations to masquerade under this protection, as "individual persons" under law. This has led to today's confusion over property rights, which no longer distinguish between the necessary inviolability of individual property rights needed to assure personal autonomy and self-reliance, self-respect and self-motivation, and the endless accumulation of property by corporations and institutions to the point where they have the power to press and disenfranchise individuals and smaller groups.

This remarkable book helps us to see today's resurgence of co-ops, neighborhood revival, community economic reconstruction and land trusts in the context of past efforts. By so doing, it helps demonstrate the irrelevance of old political labels, whether they be Republican or Democrat, Liberal or Conservative, capitalist or socialist. Decentralism is one of the keys to understanding the new politics of our time, and how some of the most interesting contemporary figures, from Jimmy Carter to Jerry Brown of California, can be interpreted.

The emerging politics of "small is beautiful" springs from a tradition as old as our nation's founding; from Thomas Jefferson to Ezra Heywood, William B. Greene, J.K. Ingals, Henry George and Josiah Warren in the

19th Century, to economic and land reformers Ralph Borsodi, Stuart Chase, Elton Mayo, Scott Nearing and other decentralists of this century, to today's convergence of apparent polar-opposites and new groups of strange bedfellows, such as the Libertarians, appropriate technology innovators, small-business people, ecology activists, holistic health-care promoters, advocates of states' rights and consumer protection, together with new labor unions for farms and household workers, advocates of worker-ownership of businesses and neighborhood economic development.

This is an invaluable book for those who wish to interpret the new politics of reconceptualization. It documents the earlier experiments and theories of decentralism, and highlights for me the reason that they were overwhelmed by the rising tide of industrialism. That faulty logic was cancelled by the cornucopia of resources which earlier, smaller populations could exploit for two centuries before the social bills began coming due. The early decentralists with their more profound ecological and social logic battled the tide and left us their precious legacy, ready for today's New Age decentralists to apply successfully in the receding backwash of the now-exhausted Industrial Era.

Reading Mildred Loomis will ensure that we waste no time re-inventing wheels.

Hazel Henderson,
Creating Alternative Futures: The Politics of Reconceptualization

Ralph Templin and
Paul Keene directed
School of Living from
1940-1945

Paul Keene,
Walnut Acres

Natural Foods,
Penns Creek, PA

J.I. Rodale (1898–1971), Emmaus, PA
Founder, Editor, and Organic Gardener

Raised Bed Gardening, Organic Farms, midseason, 1979

Ralph Borsodi
(1886-1977)

Decentralist Supreme

The School of Living, near Suffern, NY, 1936-1945

Mildred and John
Loomis

Mildred J. Loomis

Lane's End Homestead, Brookville, OH
School of Living, 1940-1970

Henry George (1839-1898)

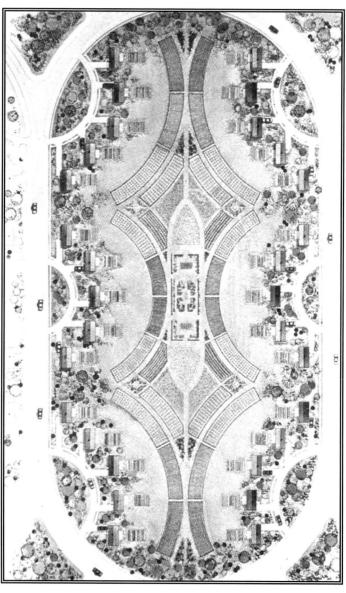

Garden Cluster Homes Community
by Raymond Pallazini, 1979

Heathcote Center, Freeland, MD
School of Living Headquarters, 1970-1976

Deep Run Farm, RD 7, York, PA
School of Living Headquarters, 1976

Dr. Arthur Morgan
(1878–1975), Founder,
Community Service, Inc.

Hazel Henderson

Ralph Borsodi and Mildred J. Loomis discuss
Education and Living with Shyam Chawla, Bombay, India, 1965

íntroÒuctíon

Americanism—Since 400,000 B.C.

A kind of negativism prevails as America moves into the 1980s. People approach the 1980s with questions, confusion, and apathy. Generally, it's recognized that the United States, both North and South, is at an ecological low. Farmers mine the soil, and miners rip up the land, leaving it open and unhealed. Forests are removed. Factories pour gases into the air and wastes into the lakes and rivers and oceans. Constantly-extended concrete and plastic jungles leave decaying cities with rejected industrial sectors. And the response is blah—masses of people embedded in the 9 to 5 routine, attending mostly to their evening TV and weekend paychecks. The "public" indifferently calls it Progress.

In this strange American bubbling and simmering, some individuals emerge and join groups to "maintain" the American dream, others to "change and improve it." Conservatives confirm—but not too confidently—faith in competition, profit, and the two-party system. Libertarians—notably intellectual and often well-to-do young people—discuss and publish the theses of F.A. Hayek, Ludwig von Mises, and Murray Rothbard. Others follow the land reform of Thomas Jefferson and Henry George; still others develop cooperatives and the integral education-and-living activities of decentralist Ralph Borsodi.

The Native Americans

Behind them are still others, the Native Americans, who look to their own pre-European cultures in America as root and direction for the future.

DECENTRALISM

They supply a depth and challenge too easily neglected as a result of the stereotypes of history and their "isolation," plus the ethnocentricity of European culture.

It behooves us to look to the heart of the Native Americanism—a way of thinking about the Universe, and the way of living that results from that philosophy. The essence of the Native viewpoint is stated in *Black Elk Speaks*:

> All creation is sacred. Every dawn is a holy event. Their light comes from your Father and the two-leggeds and all the other people who stand upon this earth are sacred and treated as such.
>
> The story of all life is old and good to tell, we two-leggeds sharing in it with the four-leggeds and the winds of the air and all green things; all are children of one mother and their father is one Spirit. Is not the sky a father and the earth a mother, and are not all living things with feet or wings or roots their children?
>
> For we Indians, there is just the Sacred Pipe, the Earth we sit on, and the open sky. The Spirit is everywhere, showing itself through an animal, a bird, some tree and hills. Sometimes it speaks from the Badlands, from a stone, from the water.
>
> If this earth should ever be destroyed, it will be by desire, by the lust of self-gratification, by greed for the green frog-skin (money), by people who are mindful only of their own self, forgetting about the wants of others.
>
> We Indians must show how to live with our brothers, not use them, or maim them. With this Pipe, which is a living part of the Earth, we cannot harm any part of her without hurting ourselves. Through this Pipe, we can make peace with our greatest enemy who dwells deep within ourselves.

Simple ideas with profound implications, raising the question, how must life be lived if all living things are relatives, brothers and sisters of the same parent, this Mother Earth?

Inter-related oneness of living is Native Americanism. Yet this nature-based integral living was overrun and, at least temporarily, overcome by Europeanism—a philosophy and culture much its opposite: messianic, authoritarian, materialistic, lacking in humanistic and spiritual values.

How distorted the history and sociology textbook record! Most people carry the image of courageous emigrants fleeing European chauvanism, monarchy, exploitation, and materialism to establish a free world on a "new continent"—America, Land of the Free!

But America was free long before the Europeans arrived, free because of the way of life which the Native peoples had established. In reality, the Europeans may have found freedom here, but they re-established here the same exploitative factors which they fled in Europe. America became, alas, a base for, and in many cases, a replica of, the European tendencies they hoped to abandon. Some of the consequences of European culture, alien to Native Americanism, which were established by Europeans and now dominate Twentieth Century America have been listed by Jack D. Forbes, a Native American educator of the University of California at Davis:

1. The idea that any human being can "own" another living creature or "own" the earth, the sky, the water, or any natural thing;

2. The idea that any human has the right to live off the labor of another human, or off the lives of non-humans;

3. The idea that human beings and other living things, including the earth, can be used as means without regard to the rights and dignity of individual humans, animals, and plants;

4. The idea that those who control wealth should be able to determine what is printed, what is seen, and what is heard;

5. The idea that the state has a right to know and control what its citizens are thinking, saying, or doing in their private lives;

6. The idea that material wealth and a high standard of living is the most important human activity;

7. The idea that slogans of religious or ethical piety can actually replace day-to-day ethical living;

8. The general prevalence of arrogance and chauvanism expressed by and granted to persons and ideas of European derivation;

9. The messianic mania—the desire to force or high-pressure other people into conforming to the views of some "religious" or political secular unit.

This does not exhaust the Europeanism of America. Forbes lists 19 others in the Spring, 1974, issue of *Akwesasne Notes*, showing how overwhelmingly the "America" of the 1600s-1800s was ideologically, spiritually, historically and genealogically "Europeanized." Europeans coming to America refused to be Americanized or "naturalized." They wrote, colonized, and developed schools in which the central theme is European. It is difficult not to conclude that virtually every major problem faced in North America today, virtually every kind of unethical behavior, and every threat to individual dignity, freedom, and self-development, has a European origin.

Community, democracy, appropriate technology, natural foods, wholistic medicine, anti-statism were born in Native American villages, ranging from North to South and East to West. True, one can point out faults and problems, but only in America, as compared with the Europe of 1500-1700, were any truly free human societies in existence. And they were not products of any "New Age"—they had, so far as is known, been growing and developing for 400,000 years.

This book is a record of some political, economic and sociological efforts at freedom and a good life in America. In watching and evaluating them, we do well to note how they deal with and correct the nine serious charges and deposits from Europeanism. We may find among Native people the best examples of how to live in the Twenty-First Century.

1
ɑⅿⅇʀⅈⅽɑ'ꜱ ʀⅇⅴⅈⱺⱡⱳⱦⅈⱺⱬꜱ

In addition to the decentralist lifestyle of the native people of the Americas—or even perhaps *because* of their example, Europeans on this continent have responded to and followed rebels and revolutionaries for much of their 350-year history here. Today the on-going struggle between Authority and Liberty is called decentralism.

Revolution I

The first comers to Virginia and Massachusetts in the 1600s were resisting and fleeing from religious, economic, and political controls they had known in Europe. In their new country, their hosts were not oppressive, and they enjoyed freedom. They built homes on the land with the land's materials. They developed communities and towns. Separation from their foreign rulers by distance and oceans, along with ample land in America, their freedom seemed guaranteed. They were little troubled by "colonial status" in the first hundred years, until excise and other taxes levied by European heads of government became burdensome.

Then, stirred and guided by people such as Tom Paine, the colonists revolutionized their thinking. They would *form* their *own* government; they would write out their *own* rights to free speech, free press, free assembly, and form a constitution to outline the *limited* duties of their elected officials! They declared their independence from King George, dumped taxed tea into Boston Harbor to symbolize rejection of unwanted authority, and they defended themselves with bullets against the British Army. These shots were heard round the world. As the thirteen colonies

1

separated from England's monarch, their Declaration of Independence and Constitution of the United States of America rang from rebels and revolutionaries. With them, a citizenry had achieved their cherished voice in government.

"Liberty," the people said, "has been won!" In song and prose, in books and history, this was repeated in the following years, until everyone, in and outside the United States, believed that Americans were freed.

And so they were in a political sense—more free than before their Revolution of Independence. Now they voted and helped form laws to govern themselves. They elected delegates to legislative bodies to represent them. They decided the size and duties of their government—the one agency to which they granted the legal power to use coercion on them. Hopefully, they would forever restrain this legal power to the enforcement of their human rights, and to the protection from those who would harm their person or property.

Revolution II

Having attained their "freedom," Americans turned their muscle, zest and intelligence to their second revolution—the farming of the land, producing food, manufacturing and distributing goods, the creating of money and banks, the exporting and importing of materials.

New machines and processes were invented. Crops flowed in from fertile farms: corn, wheat, meat, milk, vegetables, fruit, cotton and tobacco. Coal and metals were mined, oil drilled, ores smelted, brick and pottery fired. Factories and foundries yielded lumber for homes, factories, ships. Endless miles of rails were laid. Schooners, trains, boats transported American goods around the globe. The land of the free was spearheading its second revolution—a technological and Industrial revolution.

Thousands of immigrants came. They were told it was the land of inexhaustible resources—forever-productive soil, forests, mines. As the ambitious and oppressed of Europe arrived, businesses flourished, cities grew and wealth piled up.

Undergirding America's second revolution were the spiritual values of Calvinism, Puritanism, and the Protestant ethic. Sloth was a sin, work a virtue. Everything sustained an unquestioned faith in mass-factory techniques. Given a seemingly boundless Earth, imaginative minds, and ever more people, no end was in sight nor imagined for the new Industrial Age.

Yet ghettos appeared in the cities, slums and shanties in the countryside. Workers sweated out long days in hot foundries, endured tiresome hours at factory benches, grumbled at sun-up to sun-down work on wheat and cotton farms. Economic depressions, bank failures and panics upset each decade. Mortgaged farms were foreclosed; urban workers were thrown out of work. They protested, besieging employers for jobs, pressuring factory owners for higher wages. Labor and capital were at loggerheads.

Revolution III

By the middle of the 1800s, came a crucial test of the American Way. The country had developed into three sections—each with a separate economy, with a class which controlled the economics also controlling the politics. Industry and finance dominated the Northeast. The planters of cotton, sugar and tobacco dominated the South. The diversified farmers had the West. The agrarian West sold its products to the financial Northeast. The plantation owners of the South, relying on African men and women as slaves (i.e., property) preferred to be left alone.

By 1860, the economic rivalry between the North and the South brought on the Civil War, with slavery a secondary but basic issue. The political Constitutional Union Party urged national unity; the Republicans nominated Abraham Lincoln to unite the major groups. Southern leaders urged secession or withdrawal from the Union if Lincoln were elected. When that happened, South Carolina, followed by six others and later five more states, withdrew and established the Southern Confederacy. Four years of bloody war followed before the National Government was restored.

In 1865, President Lincoln proclaimed it illegal to treat human beings as property. Slavery was abolished. A third and moral revolution—with economic roots—had been achieved.

DECENTRALISM

In the following half century, business, industry and technology expanded, pushing toward the unquestioned goal of more production, an ever-expanding economy, endless growth. Four practices—paper money, centralized banking, the invention of the airplane, and belt-line mass production greatly facilitated what was proudly acclaimed as "Progress." Now America was geared not only to an ever-higher standard of living for her own people, but also to feed the hungry of the rest of the world. More and more must be produced. Everyone must work harder. Surpluses piled high.

Industry and industrialism—meaning everybody—grew more and more dependent on expansion and increased production of material goods. Of material goods, along with peoples' desire for them, so the argument went, there was no end. The Siamese twins, technology and industrialism, brought ever higher material standards of living. And a higher standard of material living was, in everyone's thinking, the chief, if not the only, component of Progress. The almost unanimous conclusion at the turn of the century, and continuing through the Thirties and Forties, was that Progress would insure the Good Life for everyone.

Perceptive observers, nonetheless, were disquieted with the underlying trend in American history. Industrial, financial, occupational, social, political, and educational affairs had all proceeded in the same direction. All had used the same method—Centralization. All were motivated by much the same value system—that happiness lay in the proliferation of material things.

Centralization is the operation of activities (of whatever type) in which control is concentrated in the hands of fewer and fewer individuals. Centralization had dulled the American dream of security and liberty.

Centralization had proceeded in seven specific areas: 1) production, 2) ownership, 3) control, 4) education, 5) government, 6) population, 7) communication. To recognize these Centralizations, to understand their nature, to evaluate their results in human and spiritual terms, is to see the need of, and possibility for, a Fourth Revolution in American affairs.

ameríca's centralízatíons
base for a decentralíst revolutíon

O f the seven Centralizations, the most important is the change from small-scale production to large factory production. It is important because the powerful forces struggling for dominance—Capitalists and Marxists—both assume the greater efficiency of large-scale production in all things over small-scale production.

Capitalism was launched on its conquering career by acceptance of Adam Smith's idea of centralization in factories, along with the efficiency of unending division of labor. Karl Marx based his idea of "scientific" Socialism upon it. Every financier and every advocate of government and economic planning postulated their programs on not only the efficiency of Industrialism, but on its inevitability and desirability. All kinds of centralization were considered progressive largely because it was assumed that centralized factories were the only efficient method of production.

At the beginning of the Nineteenth Century, both agricultural and mechanical production were carried on in farms, shops, and small plants. Mills located on streams, driven by water power, kept production localized and in many places. With the coming of the steam engine, production shifted to fewer factories where power was supplied by boilers and steam engines. Larger and larger units were constructed around the boilers, fueled by coal. Lumber was cut, ores smelted, steel produced in huge mills. People gathered to live nearby to work and produce in factories.

DECENTRALISM

In 1850, 468 iron works and steel mills supplied annually an average of $43,000 per plant to serve 23 million people. Ninety years later, in 1940, 334 steel mills produced an average of $10,000,000 worth of steel per plant for 132 millions of people. With the forming of the U.S. Steel Corporation in 1901, that industry became centralized in Pittsburgh and nearby centers.

A similar growth and centralization occurred in cotton goods, woolen clothing, in farm implements and machinery. Whereas shoes were formerly made by custom shoemakers and cloth was woven by local weavers, in the late 1800s and early 1900s, shoes and cloth came to be manufactured in large factories and mills in a few favorably-located cities.

In the 1850s, grist mills ground flour and meal in every community. Every farm and region raised its own grain. After 1875, millers were responding with large-scale production of refined and bleached white flour processed in huge centralized mills. Growing of wheat was shifted from many small farms to giant farms in Kansas and other Western states.

By 1930, the production of food, clothing, furnishings and machinery had moved into large centers. The largest industry then, manufacturing of automobiles, dominated Detroit. Increasingly, modern industry put production first and human beings second.

Centralization of Ownership—Proletarianism

Companion to centralization of place and production in factories was the centralization of ownership. Prior to 1875, businessmen had largely owned their own means of production. Farmers owned and operated their own farms; retailers owned and ran their own stores; manufacturers owned and managed their own factories. A hundred years later, ownership had been largely centralized.

From 1825 to 1920, the percentage of farms operated by their owners had been cut in half, declining about 4% per year. By 1970, three-fourths of the land was owned by others than those who lived on it and cultivated it.

The share of the national wealth held by the richest 1% of the people in the United States in 1974 is revealing: 91.6% of all trust funds and

50.8% of all corporation stocks are owned by the richest 1%, whose total net worth was $367,500,000,000. As it was stated in 1941 by the Temporary National Economic Committee after an exhaustive survey:

> The wealth and income of the country is owned by a few corporations, which in turn are owned by an infinitesimally small number of people. The profits from these corporations go to a very small group, with the result that the opportunities for new enterprises, whether corporate or individual, are constantly restricted.

Several factors influenced the centralization of ownership. One was the support of thinkers, economists, and leaders. Robert S. Brookings of Brookings Institute voiced a typical attitude and program:

> The best means of hastening the present slow and harrowing process of agricultural regimentation is by forming agricultural corporations which will accomplish in organization and management what big business has accomplished for industry. Following the method in the U.S. Steel Corporation, the most efficient farms (which as now operated are worth less than nothing) would be paid for in safe bonds of the agricultural corporation with some regard for their potential value...The efficient managers would become department managers of the corporation. These corporations would combine all the advantages claimed by Campbell and Ford for large-unit farming, with the additional advantages of efficient management. They would greatly reduce the cost of farming. Their securities would eventually become one of the most extensive and safe investments for our people.

This outright centralist philosophy and method was furthered by World War II. Thousands of small farmers and businessmen in every line of enterprise were crushed out by the hundreds of thousands. War contracts helped centralize the business of the nation in its large corporations.

Centralizing ownership of land, property, and factories into fewer and fewer hands meant transforming individual owners into wage- and salary-earners, totally dependent upon others for their employment and livelihood. Since the 1930s, the American middle-class has been educated and conditioned to acquire insurance, and if possible, enough securities to live comfortably in old age. The masses of American workers were encouraged to become dependent upon labor unions and government social security. The masses are no longer, even in theory, supposed to make themselves independent by acquiring property. They are not even expected to save enough (in bank deposits, life insurance, or investments) to meet the hazards of life and the inabilities of old age. Instead, they are trained to turn to an elaborate government social security system to deal with all life's events.

In effect, Classical Capitalism, with its emphasis on the widespread ownership of property and exchange via the free market has changed into Absentee or Finance Capitalism, rapidly tending toward State Capitalism. While centralists validate their goals and methods in terms of "increased efficiency," both leaders and the masses are dismayed with the current results of rapid inflation and rising unemployment.

Capitalization—The Centralization of Control

Ownership of a building may be a fact; ownership of bonds or shares of stock may be but fiction or the "shell" of a fact. Control, on the other hand, is decidedly a fact. To be able to say "I control" is to say "I have the power which ownership implies." Owners of securities may say, "I own" without being able to say, "I control." They have merely a legal token of ownership.

Corporations make it possible for some people to control property without ownership, and for others, ownership without control. In the U.S. Steel Corporation, a handful of financiers control but do not own its assets. Two hundred thousand stockholders own, but do not control, those assets. Other millions of indirect owners—bondholders, insurance policy holders, depositors in banks—whose savings the corporation invests, have even less control.

The corporation itself holds, in a kind of "trust," vast properties—land and mines, railroads and ships, factories and steel plants, coal, ore, steel, finished products and supplies of all kinds. In legal theory, the ultimate ownership of all this "property" belongs to the stockholders who are assured in annual reports that this is "your" corporation, that the directors and managers represent "you," and that the property is administered for "your" benefit.

In practice, the control of the corporation is centralized in a small group of individuals over whose activities the "owners" (both direct and indirect) have little or no control or influence. Owners may vote in the selection of these controllers, but in reality, controllers of the corporation are virtually a self-perpetuating minority who can administer the property and dispose of its earnings and capital as they think best for their own interests.

The modern business corporation (of which U.S. Steel is one of the most conspicuous) is a device used by promoters (investment bankers) to permit the capitalization of capital (machinery and buildings) and land into capital stock and securities—common and preferred shares—and debentures, bonds, etc. While this could be a useful function in a complex economy, it fails to be useful today because of the special privileges conferred by law upon incorporators, privileges which are denied to natural persons and partnerships.

Real persons are liable for any debts incurred in their transactions. But by law, the officers and incorporators of corporations are exempt from this obligation. Because of it, corporation officials can expand and take risks. If transactions are unprofitable, they can declare bankruptcy, and become exempt from personal liability for the corporation's debts. (Ostensibly, this "special privilege" was granted to encourage the accumulation of large sums for massive business undertakings.)

- Corporation officials reserve to themselves control and decision-making regarding the stock-shares and deposits made by member-investors.
- Corporations engage in "stock waterings." They purchase enterprises at one price, and capitalize them (sell stock shares) at much higher prices. They manipulate securities on the stock exchange—selling long or short on the basis of inside information.
- They pay themselves high salaries and bonuses from corporate profits.

- They pyramid all these activities through "holding corporations."
- Corporations now "integrate," owning and controlling a whole series of enterprises from production to the consumer. Tenneco can plow fields it owns with its own tractors, fueled with its own oil. It sprays its own crops with its own pesticides, and uses its own food additives. It processes its food in its own plants, packages them in containers it has manufactured, and distributes them to its own grocery stores through its own marketing systems. In its 1969 reports, Tenneco listed a gross oil income of $464 million and a taxable oil income of $88.7 million—yet due to federal tax breaks, Tenneco not only paid no taxes on that income, but had a tax credit of $13.3 million.

In *The Modern Corporation and Private Property*, Berle and Means stated that 200 of the largest corporations in the U.S. owned $150 billion worth of property. This represents control of 53% of all corporate wealth (other than banking) in the United States, 45% of all business wealth, and 25% of the entire national wealth. To add to this the savings of people in banks, plus the notes, mortgages, and other collateral given to banks to secure their loans, the centralization of control reaches unfathomable levels.

In Fascist Italy and National Socialist Germany, ownership was considered unimportant, but control was quite important. Individuals and corporations were permitted to retain title to their property and to operate their businesses. But control was taken out of their hands by semi-public officials in industry-wide cartels prescribing in detail how the owners were to operate, and what they were to do with the proceeds of their "own" enterprises. In Soviet Russia, individual control was disposed of by forbidding private enterprise altogether, and centralizing all ownership and control in the State.

Standardization—The Centralization of Education

When instruction is given by one person to another (parent to child), education is widely decentralized. It is somewhat centralized when a teacher has a class of thirty children. It is further centralized when many small schools are consolidated into one larger one, and further centralized when methods, textbooks, and curriculum are prescribed by state boards or national departments of education. When education's goals (the national cultural pattern) are set in New York, Paris, London or Moscow, centralization is almost complete. When this last process is made compulsory by law, the ultimate in centralization of education is reached.

The result is that one can now travel from one end of the enormous U.S. to the other and find uniformity in foods, clothes, stores, newspapers, factories, homes, cities. Individual, family, local, and regional influences which conflict with accepted standards are eliminated.

When people believe that Progress is the purpose for which human beings should live, and if Progress is identified with expansion of Industrialism, then the whole population must be taught to want the things and live the life which centralized industry alone can produce and provide. What economists call human wants (and advertisers call consumer demand) must be standardized until everybody wants the standardized products of industry, and is willing to live the standardized life of an industrial population.

Individuals must be taught, and re-taught, with every change in fashion and in technology, to want what industry produces for them. Leaders of industry must concern themselves with both juvenile and adult education. Industry can ill-afford to permit any institution to prefer other values than the material values which it alone is capable of supplying. Religion with emphasis on other-worldly values must be neutralized. Patriotism and conservation of civic values must be tempered. Education from the kindergarten to the university must forego any desire to teach the truth—it must concentrate on preparing the young for life in industrialized society. Industry must take the initiative. In America, its specific device for standardization is Advertising and Selling.

A whole population cannot be brought to a single classroom for indoctrination. But "education" in the way of advertisements can be taken to the people—to reach the old and young, literate and illiterate, rich and poor, urban and rural. The only useful method is one that produces results—creates demand for the products of specific manufacturers. The largest single group of individuals teaching in America are the salesmen and distributors of the products of American industry. Their role is shown by considering that the total sum expended for schooling at all levels plus that spent by religious bodies is only a small percentage of the sum spent on advertising and selling.

According to the *Sales Manager's Handbook*, more than four times is spent on advertising and selling than is spent on the nation's entire school system. Thus parents, teachers, and ministers work in a world saturated by Advertising and Selling—by those who persuade the public to do what is industrially profitable, and to want what furthers material Progress.

Advertisers teach and influence human wants from birth to death. Baby foods are sold to mothers who have been taught by advertisers to substitute them for breast-feeding. Ceremonies surrounding death reflect what is taught by modern casket and funeral industries. No bizarre method or extreme cost deters advertisers from influencing thousands of human wants.

Two examples. During the 1976 U.S. Bicentennial, a birthday cake weighing 69,000 pounds (26,000 pounds of sugar) sat on a barge in Baltimore Harbor. It had been assembled pound-cake by pound-cake inside a huge plywood shell. The shell was covered with icing and the cake set sail before thousands of delighted spectators, who later accepted pieces as mementos. Thus did Amatar Company advertise its wares and "educate" the public.

One large oil company spent one million dollars for an extravaganza between halves of the 1976 New Year's Army and Navy football game. They hired a 200-piece band, sixty comely marching cheerleaders, movie stars ensconced in flower-covered floats, and a single child carrying a sparkler. All this to later din into American ears the brand name of its gasoline on a 30-minute TV show.

The Media's Part in Centralized Education
For their daily news, most Americans read one of 1,764 newspapers, turn on a house or car radio, and sit for hours before The Tube. As with the supermarket or auto industries, the print and electronic media are being increasingly centralized. Today, all but 500 belong to one of the 167 newspaper chains, now absorbing 50 to 60 papers a year. In 1979, four

such chains predominate, raising questions of monopoly ownership, concentrated power, and the deeper question of free speech and how people get news and facts to inform their decisions.

Gannett is the largest chain, owning 78 dailies and working to control an even 100. It now reaches 3,000,000 readers daily—more than the combined daily audience of the *New York Times*, *Los Angeles Times*, and the *Washington Post*. In 1906, F.E. Gannett, a farmer's son, climbed to the editorship of the Ithaca, New York, *Daily News*. He bought a nearby newspaper, and in 51 years acquired 30 more and a string of radio and television stations. After his death, Gannett Company went public, increasing both readers and earnings. Gannett stock spiraled from $6.87 a share in 1967 to over $43 in 1979.

The Gannett chain has stiff competition from Knight-Ridder, the owner of 32 dailies, and a circulation of 3.5 million, operating large city dailies—the *Miami Herald*, the *Philadelphia Inquirer*, and the *Detroit Free Press*, with posted revenues of $879 million in 1978.

The Newhouse combine, the personal preserve of Samuel I. Newhouse, is known as "the money factory." It publishes 29 small papers (3,281,000 combined circulation) in addition to some magazines (*Vogue*, *Mademoiselle*, *House and Garden*, *Glamour*) with revenue of one billion and profits somewhere near $100 million.

"A mighty fortress and bulwark of conservatism," says N.R. Kleinfield in *New York Times Magazine* (April 9, 1979),

> …is the Tribune Company, owner of the *Chicago Tribune*, the New York *Daily News*, and seven other dailies (3.1 million circulation; revenue $967 million). Recently, the group has become an aggressive acquirer of papers which do not have competition in the cities in which they are located.
>
> Another chain acquiring other papers is the Scripps-Howard; its 17 dailies are read by 1.8 million people in cities like Cincinnati, Cleveland, and Denver. Informed sources put revenues at about $425 million.

DECENTRALISM

The Hearst Corporation is a reviving empire with 10 dailies (1.4 million circulation) and *Harpers Bazaar*, *Good Housekeeping*, *Cosmopolitan*. Revenues at $400 million. Notorious for forging its papers into political weapons. Hearst has lately been letting its editors take charge.

Other powers include the well-fixed Dow Jones & Co., fueled and expanded by the wealthy *Wall Street Journal*; Times-Mirror, parent of the *Los Angeles Times*; the *Washington Post*; and of course, the New York Times Company, which has 5 weeklies and 9 dailies in Florida and North Carolina in addition to the *Times*. Last year, the Dow Jones Company took in $481,558,000.

Where does this leave the readers of newspapers? What about the people's right to know? To some extent this has to do with the editor's right to edit. It all brings up the matter of control. Most large groups claim they grant local autonomy. But conferences are held frequently to exchange ideas, and, some say, to exercise control over policy. All publish newspapers whose main purpose is to make a profit.

As the newspaper and other media chains enlarge, the Specter of monopoly looms. Said Representative Morris Udall, Democrat from Arizona, "I really shudder to see the day when you have four or five organizations with a hammerlock on what Americans read…The day may come when such leaders hunger for political power. It could be used."

A member of an investment firm said, "Papers will become more homogenized. They'll look and read alike. Newspapers are going to have less personality. They're becoming more service-oriented—especially the chain newspapers with their sophisticated marketing approach. You'll see fewer gadflies."

Does a newspaper have an obligation to educate its readers?

"There's a difference between what readers want and need," said the present head of Gannett's. "Predominantly we give them what they want, a smaller proportion of what they need."

Nationalization—The Centralization of Government

The essence of society is people; of nation, territory; of government, coercion. The U.S. government in Washington, democratic as it is supposed to be, is not the people in the United States, nor is it the rich land between the oceans, nor is it a mystical national entity supposed to combine both land and people. Government is that group of officials distinguished by the fact that they and they only have the legal right to exercise authority over the territory, and use coercion on the people within its boundaries.

Centralization of government means 1) the shifting of activities from local officials to national officials; 2) increasing the number of public officials of all kinds; and 3) actual increase of legal coercion in dealing with problems people face. Since the 1930s, six types of activities have been increasingly taken over by Washington because 1) people believe federal control is more efficient; 2) to assure equalization of public service throughout the country, and in some cases, 3) to deal with a national emergency.

Six nationalized activities include:

1. *Political*: In America, nationalization does not abolish state and local officials—local ones continue to perform to a lesser extent. Some political activities once considered primarily state and local and now recognized as national are law enforcement, construction of public improvements; regulation of banks, railroads, ex-changes, corporations, etc; public relief; social security; controlling labor relations. Whereas in 1920 there were 156 federal bureaus, in 1977 there were over 12,000. One hears less and less of "states' rights" and "local autonomy."

2. *Social*: Activities once performed by charitable and philanthropic organizations, by professional and trade associations, by labor unions, by private, school, library, museum and similar institutions, are now done by federal bureaus.

3. *Individual:* People no longer look to themselves to obtain employment, but to government. Recreational facilities are not provided by individual and family action, but by the "public." Even vital needs cease to be privately provided, as the government provides housing, schools, child care, homes for the aged, and school lunches. With total centralization, as

15

in Soviet Russia, all individual activities become nationalized and public officials provide facilities for work, play and rest. Thus public officials inescapably prescribe what all individuals shall do.

4. *Ownership of Property*: Government administration and ownership of property begins reasonably with the regulation of banks, railroads, power companies, public utilities, mining, forestry and other natural resources. But soon, the difference between public and private property is ignored, and regulation changes to intervention by public officials into the operation of private enterprises. This goes farther into government ownership of whole industries—banking and mining in Britain, and in Soviet Russia the nationalization of all industries whatsoever.

5. *Medical Services*: Distinction between public and private health is important. Logic supports the use of governmental coercion to deal with epidemics, infectious disease, to enforce quarantine, protect water supply, inspect restaurants. But government goes farther into private health by licensing physicians, employing physicians in government health services and hospitals, granting workman's compensation, and ending with the socialization of all medicine. With total nationalization, not only medicine, but also health, becomes a matter of national and official concern, not individual concern.

6. *Education*: Nationalization of the school system begins with the idea that voters must be intelligent in order to select wise officials—hence the education of the young is a civic concern. Everyone is compelled to support schools which every child must attend. Schools, originally, were private, and then came to be established and controlled by local officials and boards. On the plea of efficiency, their control is shifted to state supervisors and departments. On the plea of equalizing educational opportunities, control shifts to the national government.

Nationalization of education seems to prevent the communication of ideas that have not been officially approved. Anything anti-official is suppressed. The official doctrines and propaganda are imposed on everybody. In addition, to the extent that government officials license halls and eating places, control the use of the post office, telephone and radio, or acquire control of printing and paper, the foundation is laid for disseminating official propaganda and preventing circulation of anti-official sentiments. Only the American belief in free speech and assembly holds censorship somewhat in abeyance.

Comparing population and government employees reveals the extent of nationalization. In 1816, there was one civil servant (including the military) to every 1,336 persons. By 1950, there was one person governmentally-employed to every 44 persons in the country, and if armed services and state and local government employees are added in, there was in 1950 one government employee for every four families (16 persons) in the United States.

Urbanization—The Centralization of Population

In industrial nations, people have been concentrating on smaller and smaller areas of land, with resulting depopulation of the rural areas, and over-population of cities.

In 1960, the U.S. continental area was 3,628,150 square miles, on which lived 183,285,000 people, or an average density of 41 persons per square mile. Of course, 41 persons did not live on every square mile; the density in specific areas gives a truer picture. Nevada had an average density of one person per square mile; Rhode Island 674, and Ohio 163 persons per square mile.

In cities, of course, the density intensifies. In the New York Metropolitan District (2,154 square miles), the pro-rated density is 4,336 persons per square mile, but the density of New York City itself is 23,178. The congestion increases in a model housing project with 50,659 persons per square mile. Thus in one square mile of New York City in 1960 were crowded more people than the whole of New York City's 1800 population: 49,401.

In 1890, 57% of the total U.S. population lived in strictly rural areas; by 1930, it had declined by one-third, or 36.4%. Each census since then has reported more people moving from rural to urban areas than has returned to the country. In 1975, for the first time in history, more people left American cities than entered them to reside there.

DECENTRALISM

By way of seven Centralizations, modern America by the 1970s had reached an epitome of Progress and Affluence. Concrete and stone were layered, level upon level, until buildings towered a hundred stories into the air. Vast cities stretched along both East and West seacoasts. In between, each state was building to match Chicago. Subway tunnels burrowed into the earth, and tracks were elevated to transport millions of people speedily between their jobs and their homes. People communicated instantly across continents by telephone, radio, and TV. The Quantity Age came to be with us.

How about Quality? Are people more satisfied? Are they happier surfeited with things, than in an earlier day of simpler living? Has Centralization served them well?

To answer these questions, one must have a standard—a criterion—from which to rate and judge life in the modern day. Here I use several tests—economic, ethical, the psychological, physiological, and esthetic—by which to test the results of the seven Centralizations. I assume, with Ralph Borsodi who established and researched pertinent tests in 1928-1945, that normal human beings are able to, and do, support themselves; that they are able to bear and nurture healthy young, and that both adults and children are physically and mentally healthy; that they do not commit crime; that they enjoy beauty, and that their producing/making of things is satisfying and artistic. In brief, normal human beings avoid dependency, delinquency, disease, degeneracy, and decadence.

How Centralization Rates On The Tests

Dependency: Dependency is the state of those who receive their food, clothing, and shelter from others. Dependency of young children on parents is normal; dependence of healthy adults on others for maintenance is abnormal. Persons earning their maintenance are also dependent if they have no alternative to their employment—if they have no savings or property; if they are subject to arbitrary dismissal by an employer, dictation by union officials, or regimentation by government officials as to hours of work, wages, or salary.

The total of both normal and abnormal dependents includes about one-half of the whole U.S. population. Industrialism and Urbanism prevent millions of city children from contributing to self-support. Country children at ten years of age can be almost totally supporting. The number of parasitic and non-productive persons (and those who have no alternative to being employed by others) is constantly rising, while the self-supporting numbers are constantly declining.

Three trends in modern industrialism raise the number of non-workers: 1) increasing the age at which children can work, along with extending the years during which children and youth are in school; 2) lowering the age of adults for retirement; 3) urban homes becoming consuming instead of producing units. This last deprives both children and the aging of the productive work they used to perform on country farms and homesteads.

With modern industry has come increasing economic inter-dependence. Inter-dependence is good where individuals do not become parasites or lose their alternatives for self-employment.

Industrialism is constantly increasing the number of persons who distribute instead of produce. In 1870, only 3% of the population were distributors. And most of them were merchants and shopkeepers in business for themselves. In the 1970s, 40% are hauling, selling, or advertising goods. In a day of mail-order houses, of department and chain-stores, distributors are mostly sales clerks and employees entirely dependent for their livelihoods upon employment by others. An increasing proportion becomes parasitic and dependent. To whatever extent this violates human nature and involves people in frustration, it disposes them to disease, degeneracy, and delinquency.

Delinquency. Delinquency refers not merely to breaches of the law, but acts which violate society's ethical standards. Delinquency refers to habitual behavior where character is involved, not merely to commit a single or occasional act. Delinquency includes crimes against person or against property (assaults and thefts); violation of a people's moral sense (lying); imposition upon rights of others; legal acts of predation ("feather-bedding" by unions); legal exploitation (special privilege and monopoly); legal extortion (usury of investment bankers); sexual crimes and misbehavior; and improvidence.

The increase of criminal behavior in the modern world is well known. In *The Criminals We Deserve* (1937), Henry T.F. Rhodes says,

> Mass production is more than industrial technique. We mass-produce criminals too. Modern industrial society has produced the modern slum, the worst of all mass-produced articles…Great wealth has been created, but in the scramble for it, the slum remains. That contradiction is reflected in the mind and heart of the underdog. A great struggle ensues between the modern criminal and modern society. The revolt of the criminal is often a revolt against intolerable conditions.

Not all crimes are reported nor prosecuted. Criminologists assume that of every 100 crimes perpetrated, only 5 are reported, and of them, only two prosecuted. Yet recorded figures show that crime and delinquency almost doubled between 1900 and 1930, and has continued to increase since then. A summary shows that as population shifted from farms and villages to huge metropolitan centers, crime has become more and more common. The pattern seems to be "the larger the city, the greater the number of crimes."

For cities of 2,500 to 5,000, there are 736 crimes per100,000 population. For cities of 5,000 to 10,000, the figure climbs slightly to 947. For cities of 10,000 to 25,000, there are 1,014 crimes per 100,000 persons, while cities of 25,000 to 100,000 have 1,533 and cities over 100,000 an unhealthy 1,779.

Elton Mayo reports a searching analysis of the relation of urban congestion to delinquency in *Problems of an Industrial Society* in 1933. He examined the record of 6,398 male offenders (ages 17 to 20) in Chicago courts on felony charges in three years. On a special map, with Chicago's Loop as the center, it showed 25.1% as the crime rate at that spot. In eight concentric circles, each indicating a mile's distance, the rate decreased to 16.3, 15.5, 10.1, 7.5, 5.3, 4.5, and in zone 8, 3.7% on the residential periphery. Subsequent studies found this pattern repeated in Philadelphia,

Cleveland, Denver and other large cities. The nearer a residential locality is to the center of the city, the higher the rate of delinquency and crime. Mayo concluded: "The invasion of residential communities by business and industry disintegrates the community as an agent of social control. Inner compulsion imposed by social tradition on an ordered community breaks down."

In *Principles of Criminology* (1939), Edwin Hardin Sutherland shows that the great rise in modern mobility has increased crime. Seaports, resort towns, and those with transient populations have the highest crime rates, which increase with the size of the community. The same trend was evident to Sutherland, who said, "As people become more and more industrial, and they devote themselves to acquiring higher and higher standards of living, they depend less on home and family, and organize their lives more and more around social and political institutions. With it, delinquency and crime naturally increase."

Disease. Modern medical practice and sanitation have reduced the rate of blindness in America. But they have not reduced the number suffering from poor eyesight. Modern people definitely see less clearly than primitive ones. Similarly, sanitation and inoculation are credited with reduction of infectious diseases—malaria, smallpox, typhoid. Medical technology has made life tolerable—even useful and productive—for many with physical defects or blindness or deafness.

But modern, centralized civilization has produced an ailment peculiarly its own—anomie and alienation. Sociologist Durkheim maintained that in proportion as an industrial society develops, people suffer from anomie—a restlessness that turns to apathy. In a small society (or society of small groups), life is ordered so that the interests of its members contribute to the group. During infancy and adolescence, an individual sees ahead how he will function when he is adult. This anticipation regulates his thought and action, and culminates in adult satisfaction in being useful and necessary to his group. Since modern life does not supply this training and experience, planlessness and anomie result. Happiness lies beyond present achievement; defeat turns to disillusionment, and to disgust with the "futility of endless pursuit."

Degeneration. Moreover, modern life has brought a terrifying increase in physical and mental degeneration—heart trouble, diabetes, muscular dystrophy, cancer, psychopathology, drug addiction, sexual perversion, sterility and insanity. One in four Americans in the 1970s is developing cancer, and one-third of those will die from it. Stress, devitalized food, isolated sedentary living all contribute to lack of resistence and degenerative disease in modern America. Obviously, some defectives are unavoidable in any population, but in a normal healthy society, their percentage would be low, and the rate would not rise. The statistics from a typically modern industrialized area (New York State) show the reverse. The rate of insanity per 100,000 persons increased steadily from 1850 (67.3) to 1880 (183.3) to 1931 (273.0) to 1942 (364.2). Similarly, the number of patients per 100,000 people who are in New York mental hospitals increased from 1889 (260.4) to 1927 (422.5) to 1940 (637.6) to 1970 (2,481)!

Benjamin Malzburg in *Social and Biological Aspects of Mental Disease* (1940) said,

> Approximately one person out of twenty-two becomes a patient of mental disease during a generation…One out of six born after 1950 will spend a part of his life in a mental institution. At this rate, by the year 2000, one of every two persons will experience mental disease.

The rate of insanity in cities is twice as high as in rural America. Mayo's Chicago map plotted for crime shows a similar pattern for insanity—the rate near the Loop was the highest, and the decline was proportional toward the periphery.

Rates for suicide (total escape from living) are equally indicative. Suicides are 50% higher per capita in urban than in rural areas, with the rate on the increase.

Decadence in Work and Art: How satisfying is the work of modern people, and the things they produce? How satisfying is their play and leisure activities?

If work is satisfying, it is so because it uses all the aspects of the person working—it uses his whole being, his body, mind and will. A man is making a chair. He uses his mind to design it; his will to decide that it is for his wife's comfort; he carefully chooses his materials and tools. Then he executes it with his hands and muscles. Completed, it is his chair. No one gave him a pattern, saying, "Make it like this." No one handed him pine when he knew it should be oak. Only with his own sharp saw and chisel could he make a *good* chair—one that expressed his own self—he feels completed, fulfilled, satisfied.

Such integral self-expression is instinctive to human beings, strong in every normal person. Industrial work—factory work—distorts it. People become specialists, only designing, only cutting, only assembling, or only polishing. Too often workers are tenders of machines, or punchers of buttons—not so much making things as making money.

Leisure activities are likewise distorted in modern industrial society. Instead of singing or dancing to return refreshed to the work they love (as in more wholesome societies), moderns resort to watching, viewing, and consuming the activities and objects produced by others. They go to the theater, opera, sports arena, and stay glued to the TV to soothe or stimulate jaded nervous systems. Modern man works and plays in ways that degrade his nature. Whatever the origin of humans, they are creatures who know and will and love. Yet cruelty, irresponsibility, and ignorance increase. Such falling away from nature is a degradation and inhuman.

If modern Progress is a good goal for which human beings should live, then as people industrialize, urbanize, and centralize, five results should lessen. There should be less restriction on decision-making; less dependency, disease and degeneration, less delinquency and decadence. That these five D's are ever present and on the increase in modern society calls for a Fourth Revolution—a decentralist revolution.

Decentralization is not a turning back of the clock. Through decentralization, independence would replace dependency; honesty and justice would replace delinquency. Health would prevent disease and degeneracy; creative work and folk art would replace decadent and inhuman activities.

23

DECENTRALISM

For these desired ends, Decentralization would organize production, control, ownership, government, communications, education, and population in smaller, more human units.

Such a trend is apparent as we move into the 1980s. The worm is turning. Important groups and wise individuals have contributed to decentralist ends and means in American history. Some have worked significantly and dropped out of sight. Others continue, more or less obscurely. Most of them have been crowded out of school textbooks, and hidden from public discussion by the all-conquering Centralization of modern times. But as the 1980s begin, hundreds of thousands of people are seeking human alternatives. Thousands of groups are publishing journals, exchanging newsletters, and getting into action over environmental, social, political, energy, and many other issues. Knowledge, support, and guidance are at hand in American decentralist forebears. In the following chapters, I present five groups and outstanding leaders who comprise America's fourth and decentralist revolution.

These groups will include America's early voluntarists or individualist-anarchists, headed by Josiah Warren; the land-reformers led by philosopher/economist Henry George; the decentralists guided by Ralph Borsodi and the School of Living; the cooperators first launched by the Rochdale weavers in 1844; and the Libertarians, spearheaded by Murray Rothbard and Milton Friedman.

3
individualists: replacing government with voluntary action

I n modern society, people everywhere are born into an area "ruled"by some government. By law, citizens at their maturity become supporting, tax-paying members of that government. Attempts to withdraw, or failure to pay support-taxes, result in imprisonment or fine. Had Americans insisted on Jefferson's view that "government is an evil to be watched like fire," instead of becoming Centralists they would have held government to its one legitimate function of protecting life, liberty and property when they are threatened with harm.

Americans have other mentors in replacing government with voluntarism, mentors who went even further than Jefferson toward liberty and voluntary action. I present them first because their comprehensive challenge against centralism surfaced *before* other Fourth Revolutionaries came on the scene.

From about 1790 to 1930, America produced a group who believed, taught, and demonstrated that *all* human activities and all organizations should be voluntary—that even defense need not be governmental and coercive. They worked hard to free the economy of monopoly and exploitation in order that crime would be reduced, and the need for defense would fall to a minimum.

Persons holding these beliefs and practices sometimes call themselves "individual anarchists." Examining the root meaning of "anarchy," we find that "an" means no or none, "archy" means rulership. Thus "anarchy" means no rulership or *enforced* authority. Anarchy does not mean chaos and disorder. Such misunderstanding and misuse of the term stems from the 1886 Haymarket affair in Chicago, when workers in the McCormick Harvester Corporation were on strike. In a public demonstration supporting the strikers, someone threw a bomb. Several policemen and bystanders were killed. In spite of pleas of innocence, eight anarchists were indicted. Still today, persons who have professed anarchism are not eligible for immigration or entry to the United States.

Today, the terms *anarchist*, *anarchism*, and *anarchy* have been used so loosely that their specific meaning of no *enforced* authority has been obscured. Anarchists do, of course, believe in authority, and in leadership, and in organization—all voluntary and unimposed. It is an error to use "anarchy" to mean chaos, or hostility to the status-quo.

True anarchists hold that individual choice is primary to maturity and responsibility. For this, they hold that private property is essential, i.e., for courageous dissident beliefs or actions, a person must be beholden to no one—neither to employer nor group or government. For such independence, he needs a place of his own, inviolable and private to himself, from which he can produce his own survival, and from which he cannot be excluded for speech or actions that harm no one. To ensure widespread private property, individualist anarchists work to remove all forms of privilege and monopoly which centralize property, ownership, and control into the hands of a few people.

From 1800 to 1925, America produced a group of sturdy individualist anarchists who adhered to decentralized local communities, and free association of producers and consumers in urban centers. They abandoned the ideal, of an *equalitarian* utopia where everyone was an *economic equal* under pooled property. Instead, they worked for a world of *equity*—a world free of legal privilege and free from legal restrictions to opportunity to work and live.

Josiah Warren (1798–1874)

First in time and in scope of his efforts was Josiah Warren. A New England musician and inventor, he joined the trek west in 1819 to better his economic condition. He settled in Cincinnati and might have become a wealthy man, had not Robert Owen's cooperative colony at Harmony, Indiana, impressed him with its social reform.

Robert Owen assumed that human nature was a constant, with man's character and behavior resulting from outside environmental forces. Consequently, desirable conduct would result from good societal influences. In Scotland, Owen had already developed unsurpassed living and working conditions in his factory, and wanted to extend such in the new continent. From its Rappite owners, Owen purchased the Harmony, Indiana, colony, renamed it New Harmony, and brought in settlers sympathetic to his ideas, including equality of income.

Josiah Warren joined the group and helped draft the Constitution of New Harmony, Community of Equality. But New Harmony was short lived. Due to Owen's absence on business abroad, and to a basic error in principle, said Warren, New Harmony died out in two years. Warren also blamed its demise on the submergence of the individual within the community. "Not only was individual initiative stifled, but the elimination of personal property rights resulted in almost full loss of *responsibility*—for incapacity, failure, and shortcomings of all kinds." "Our united interests were at war with our instinct for self-preservation," said Warren. "Our own inherent law of diversity conquered us."

Warren went on his own to experiment with equality of labor—an hour for an hour of labor. On May 18, 1827, he opened a retail store in Cincinnati with $300 worth of groceries and dry goods. He posted the bills of purchase so that all could see what had originally been paid for the goods on sale. A cost-price was charged, plus 7% mark-up for shipping and store overhead. For his own labor, Warren required the purchaser to give him a labor-note promising an equal amount of the customer's work. From a large clock, all could see the time spent in exchange. Called "The Time Store," Warren was gratified with its success, and a few other merchants undertook the plan.

DECENTRALISM

Warren's further goal, however, was to establish a community on voluntary individualist principles. A delay in forming a full-fledged mutualist colony led Warren to complete his proof press with which to print his own brand of social reform. "Printing is the power that governs the destinies of mankind," wrote Warren. "Those who control the printing press control their fellow creatures." In 1851, the first catalog of the Smithsonian Institution was printed on Warren's press.

In his *Equitable Commerce* (1847), Warren discarded all varieties of collectivism, paternalism, all political and violent revolutionary action. He defined his individualist stand, the proper reward of labor, emphasized the security of personal property, and freedom of the individual. He summed it all up in two slogans: "Sovereignty of the Individual" and "Cost, The Limit of Price."

Warren's solutions dispensed with government other than that of each person over himself. "The only ground upon which human beings can know liberty is that of disconnection and individuality." For Warren, a prerequisite of a self-sufficient society was the decentralization of manufacturers, confined to production for local needs. But Warren's chief energies went into forming communities demonstrating his principles.

In Warren's development of 400 acres in Tuscarawas County, Ohio, members built houses and a saw mill on the labor-for-labor principle. Capital was supplied without interest. In 1834, America had a full-fledged anarchist community long before anything similar was attempted in Europe. But Tuscawaras land was in a low-lying area, subject to malaria. An epidemic spread among the thirty families, and the first equity village was abandoned in 1835.

Warren spent the next ten years on inventions and publishing; his enthusiasm for new experiments continued. In 1842, he opened his second "Time Store" on the outskirts of New Harmony. Again customers exchanged labor for labor, and used the labor-note currency. Resulting price-cuts brought customers from a hundred miles around.

Warren persuaded some of the Owenites who had been at New Harmony to join him in the cost-price individualist variety of decentralization. In their new community, Utopia On The Ohio River, some one hundred residents built and operated a saw mill, a grist mill, a steam mill and a carpenter shop, using the labor-exchange ideal, the labor-note currency, and a time store, selling basic merchandise. Warrenism remained there for over a quarter of a century, while Warren's major energies swung to the East.

In New York and Boston, Warren had the intellectual stimulus of other individualists. In 1851, he began another equitist community, Modern Times, on 750 acres on southern Long Island, 40 miles from New York City. Land was sold to hand-picked settlers (at $20 an acre-lot) who in turn screened later buyers to eliminate those hostile to the cost-principle. They built homes of the gravel-lime mixture of the area. Warren erected his house for $120, and later sold it for the same sum.

Warren's concept of individuality put no restraints on personal, religious, or moral practices. That women at Modern Times wore men's clothing and bloomers was a scandal to outsiders, and was the basis for an attack on Modern Times as a center of sexual irregularity. Such charges were unfounded, and when a barrage of innuendo in New York newspapers led Warren to issue a public refutation, Modern Times could no longer continue in pleasant obscurity.

Two members of Modern Times added to the unsavory public image with their social causes. Dr. Thomas L. Nichols deplored the state's sanction of marriage, and Henry Edger, an Englishman, took up the ideas of August Comte that "only society exists—society determines individuals."

Warren deplored mixing Nichol's marriage reform with his own labor reform. Dismayed by the bad press caused by Nichols and Edger, Warren nonetheless was satisfied that Modern Times felt little shock from the economic panic of 1857. Unlike the general public, Modern Timers were not affected by the over-issue of currency. Their labor-notes were accepted in payment of taxes during the depression which followed the panic.

Crime was never a problem in Warren's Modern Times. Lack of disorder and violence in the absence of constituted authority for such a long period is a challenge to those who believe that organized society without a "ruler" is doomed to chaos.

DECENTRALISM

The only "government" Warren proposed was a system of delibera-
tive bodies, approximating courts, consisting of wise older members.
These counsellors served for the voluntary contributions from those who
used their services. The counsellors aired the citizen's disputes before all
who cared to be present. In case of civil disorder, Warren approved the use
of a group trained in *preventative* techniques to use *restraint* in protecting
person or property.

The Civil War greatly increased the centralization of factories, commerce, finance and government. The anarchist aspects of Modern Times
tapered off. In 1847, Warren retired to report his ideas and experiences in
Equitable Commerce. Further efforts and writings of anarchists fell to a significant group of Warren's disciples.

Ezra Heywood (1833–1893)

A native of Westminster, Massachusetts, and a graduate of Brown University, Ezra Heywood was vigorously involved in the anti-slavery movement. Meeting Josiah Warren persuaded him to search for the causes of
poverty. Gradually, he gave up belief in political action and formed the
New England Labor Reform League to work for "free contracts, free
money, free markets, free transit, free land—by discussion, petition, re-
monstrance and the ballot to establish these articles of common need and
common right."

Heywood moved to Princeton and established the Cooperative Publishing Company, the center of anti-statist publications for over a decade.
Its *Declaration of Sentiment of the Reform League* has few equals for change
of the existing American society. Land, including all minerals, was to be
held as common property; opportunity was open to all individuals to use
and occupy such resources during their lifetimes, rather than communal
use. Tariffs were to be removed; labor-note currency should circulate in
free public markets; services of railroads, telegraph and express lines
should be provided at cost, resulting from free, open competition among
them.

In 1869, Heywood published *Yours or Mine*, showing why *occupancy
and use* of land was the only valid title to land. An individual could claim

only that land which he actually occupied and used in his own livelihood. Monopoly (ownership permitted by government) and not "society" was responsible for the rise of land values. Absolute ownership of land in excess of its use created the inequality of wealth. A second cause was the "exclusive" or monopolized currency. Both rent of land and interest on money, according to Heywood, were nothing but taxes on labor.

In *Hard Cash* (1874), Heywood wrote:

> Since money is the common measure of products, and exchange must be made in the accepted currency, it is clear that whoever controls the nature and amount and the value of this medium can tax us on our business for the actual privilege of living.

Heywood assaulted the limited economy (gold and silver) basis of money, and called for a free currency issued by a mutual (cooperative) bank. Anything that had exchangeable value was money. Since property had exchangeable value, property was suitable backing for money.

Heywood established a journal, *The Word*, and became catalyst for a group of varied reformers including Josiah Warren, Bronson Alcott, William B. Green, Lysander Spooner, some Owenites, Fourierites, and feminists. *The Word* circulated widely in America, Europe, and South Africa. Heywood taught that "government was a conspiracy of the wealthy for their own interests"; he attacked the possessors of large fortunes, the graduated tax, the abuse of the eight-hour-day law, promoted radical feminist ideas, and opposed legal marriage. Warren and others did not support Heywood in everything, but Heywood was undaunted by criticisms and suggestions.

In 1877, Heywood became the victim of Anthony Comstock interests, and was charged with circulating "obscene material" through the mail. Because of his defense of female independence, Heywood was arrested and jailed. A mass meeting of 6,000 people protested. Heywood and friends secured 70,000 signatures to a petition to repeal the Comstock laws. Released, Heywood continued working for "a union of various aspects of the intellectual radical movement" (interrupted by another jail sentence) until his death in 1893. His published works of Josiah Warren and William B. Greene are his best contributions to decentralist history.

William B. Greene, Money Reformer (1810–1878)

The panic of 1837 with its drastic curtailment of credit stirred widespread concern in economic and financial circles. Banking abuses gave rise to many proposed radical remedies. People generally feared an alliance between big bankers and politicians; they looked for solutions on a local level, by-passing large scale reforms. A drive for centralized banking was meeting opposition in that period. Into this unrest came anarchist ideas, chiefly those of William B. Greene, on money and banking, on which Warren and Heywood had been inconclusive.

Born in Haverhill, Massachusetts, in 1810, William B. Greene was educated at West Point, led a campaign against the Seminoles in Florida, but came to see war as unjust. He prepared for the ministry, and wrote religious tracts. His expositions on mutualism in banking began in the *Worcester Palladium* in 1849. Expanded as *Mutual Banking*, it became the most widely reprinted of anarchist publications on finance by an American.

Dr. James Martin, a prominent historian of American anarchy, says,

A bank in Greene's opinion had only one reason for existing—that of being a place to bring together borrowers and lenders, regardless of what capital for lending consisted, or what was wanted by the borrower. The man without tools was helpless, while the owner of such things could only watch them deteriorate if users of them could not be found. Being 'mutually necessary' to each party, banks could help bring them together.

Greene saw that banks as then constituted were not acting in the interests of the people of the community. He regarded the free competition among owners of capital as healthful, lowering the rate of interest, and thus guaranteeing to the worker a larger percentage of his production. Once a bank became organized, this process ceased. "In banks, capitalists

32

combine to prevent a fall in the price of money (the commodity they have to offer); legislatures applaud their action and grant them charters to accomplish their purpose more easily."

Greene believed that outside competition with banks would lower the interest rate. He would provide money to borrowers "at cost" as Warren suggested. His remedy for cycles of depressions and money shortage, and his alternative to the economic control of the government-chartered banking fraternity was the *mutual bank*.

Any person could become a member of the mutual cooperative bank by pledging mortgages to the cooperative on actual property. Upon this, he would be issued bills of exchange amounting to one-half the total value of the property. All members agreed to accept such paper for all payments when presented by fellow members. The member was released from his pledge when his mortgage had been redeemed.

This system was a mutual agreement to monetize other values than gold and silver to one-half the declared valuation of those other values, i.e., labor products or property. While Greene agreed with keeping silver as the *standard* of value, he extended the backing (or redemption) of money to commodities. Greene believed such money would escape the evils of both scarcity and excess of supply. It would always be worth its face value in silver dollars, because money would be *redeemable* at sight only in merchandise and services. *Banking paper would be issued on products.*

Thus, a person with only his labor to offer could easily borrow capital to engage in productive work, and thus create capital goods of his own. Mutual bank currency would be offered at cost (probably 1% of the amount loaned) but without additional interest. Said Greene:

> Mutualism operated, by its very nature, to render political government, founded on arbitrary force, superfluous. It operates to decentralize political power, to transform the State by substituting self-government. In times of economic distress, mutual money would be a bulwark against inflation and defla-

tion—citizens cannot fail disastrously, for the real property is always there, rooted in the ground.

In England in 1878, Greene's death brought to an end the career of the ablest native-born American anarchist writer on finance. Mutual banking and currency, allowing for the monetization of all durable wealth, now became the core of anti-statist finance.

J.K. Ingalls, Land Reformer (1816–1896)

Born in Swansea, Massachusetts, in 1816, J.K. Ingalls' early life was similar to that of Heywood and Greene. As a young man, he became a convinced Quaker, espoused the diet reform of Sylvester Graham, approved the Owenites and Fourierites, promoted labor-unions, joined the abolitionists. In a brief career in the ministry, he invoked scriptural admonitions against interest-taking.

In 1845, Ingalls met leading figures in the Land Reform Society, and was convinced that the money and property systems rested on "usury in land or ground rent." His interest in land limitation, in one form or another, took precedence thereafter.

To workers, he said, "You cannot be secure, no matter how high your wages, while deprived of land and a home of your own." To abolitionists he said, "Setting a man free without access to land is mockery." To the public, he said, "You fear freeing the slaves because free black men will compete with you for your jobs."

In 1849, Ingalls met Josiah Warren and other anarchists. From their ideas, he refined and extended his land reform to occupancy-and-use as the only valid title to land.

Giving up effecting reforms through legislation, Ingalls tried forming a community for a way of life freer of commercialism. In 1849, he planned his "Mutual Township" or "Cooperative Brotherhood." In 1850, he and a group began work on a site near Parkersburg, West Virginia. Although the community continued until 1865 and beyond, its social ideas tapered off to comfortable living.

Ingalls transferred his efforts to the National Land Reform Association, and worked to repeal all laws which granted titles to absentee landholders, restricting protection only to land titles based on personal occupancy and use. He wrote for Heywood's *The Word*, and other radical journals. He studied business failures and credit stringency, and accepted Green's Mutual Bank, yet he firmly held that monopolization of the land is the chief source of economic disorder and distress.

In his book, *Social Wealth*, Ingalls advanced four reasons why land should not be subject to sale: it is not a product of human labor; it is limited in amount and unable to react to "demand"; it cannot be removed and transferred; and occupancy ends with the occupant's death. Labor could claim only occupancy of land as base for title, and claim only the land's product for sale. Ingalls deplored issuing of Greenbacks by the state. His long struggle for land reform and rejection of political action for attaining it helped firmly establish tenure by occupation-and-use in anarchist teaching.

Stephen Pearl Andrews, Social Philosopher (1812–1880)
Stephen Pearl Andrews, born in Templeton, Massachusetts, took part in all phases of native anarchism. As a young lawyer in Texas, he was mobbed for his abolitionist activity. He went to London to seek a British loan to Texas to purchase and release slaves, but did not succeed.

Returned to America, Andrews wrote articles in support of cooperation and Fourierism. He met Josiah Warren in 1848, and saw the advantage of Warren's approach over "combination of interests." Andrews then restated Warren's *Equitable Commerce* in a smooth and finished document, *Science of Society*, declaring that individual sovereignty, free voluntary association, and a cost-basis of price were immutable principles. Conformity with them produces harmony in the affairs of mankind; departure from them, confusion.

Stephen Pearl Andrews had access to columns in the *New York Tribune* to discuss Warren's principles. There he wrote:

> The most serious mistake that this world has ever made is that
> of erecting an abstraction, the State, the Church, Public Moral-
> ity, into a real personality, and making it paramount to the
> will and happiness of the individual. Give up the search after

the remedy for the evils of government in more government. The road lies just the other way—toward individuality and freedom from government...Nature made individuals, not nations; and while *nations* exist, the liberties of the individual are in danger.

Andrews admitted two obstacles to completely dispensing with government—the magnitude of combined interests in which human society was already involved, and the need for an authority somewhere to restrain encroachments. Yet he maintained his interest in natural government and natural organization, i.e., the self-election or spontaneous recognition of leaders, coupled with the continuous freedom to revolt on the part of the subjects.

In spite of his commitment to abolition, Andrews found the freedom of the individual of more importance than that of the Southern States, saying, "The scientific and harmonious adjustment of capital to labor, of employee to employer, will remain long after the issue of Slavery is dead." Andrews also supported a self-regulating system of currency and banking, based directly on labor.

An English leader declared that Andrews was "probably the most intellectual man on the planet," and Benjamin Tucker, editor of *Liberty*, said "Andrew's *Science of Society* was the ablest English book ever written in defense of Anarchist principles."

Lysander Spooner, Dissident Among Dissidents ([1808–1887)

Lysander Spooner left his father's farm in Athol, Massachusetts, at age 25, to work in Worcester's registry of deeds, and to study law under two noted jurists. He practiced for seven years in Ohio, and wrote his unorthodox Deist's Reply to Alleged Supernatural Evidences in Christianity. He supported opposition to supernal authority as well as to the State.

The panic of 1837 opened his eyes to the exploitative nature of banking by private corporations, and the increasing complication from political and governmental bodies. In his *Constitutional Law Relative to Credit, Currency, and Banking*, he said, "to issue bills of credit and promissory notes for the payment of money is as much a natural right as to manufacture cotton."

The creation of compulsory legal tender, according to Spooner, was an infringement of the constitutional clause upholding the obligation of contracts. The making of a contract, he said, was an act of *real persons*, and should be restricted to such persons. "The idea of a joint, incorporeal being (i.e., corporation or government) is nothing but fiction." When profits accrued from banking operations, the individuals in whose names the chartering had taken place appeared to collect. Yet the "heads of corporations" were protected from loss. Bank charters gave individuals two advantages—one favorable to contracts, the other favorable to avoiding the responsibility of them."

In 1844, Spooner organized the private American Letter Mail Company, delivering mail between Boston, New York, Philadelphia and Baltimore, cheaper and more expeditiously than the government's service. Complaints increased over ineffective and expensive *public* mails.

Rather than improving public service and competing with Spooner's private service, Congressional action was to "put private mail service out of business." Spooner replied that Article I, Section 8, of the U.S. Constitution gave Congress the right to establish its post office, but "it did not *prohibit* individuals from doing the same." The power to establish and the power to prohibit were two distinct and separate powers.

Spooner also showed that government monopoly of mail led to excluding such materials as it wished. Limiting circulation of mail amounted to infringement on printing and selling material as well. Spooner objected to an exclusive national system of mails on both moral and economic grounds. Congress set up stiff fines for carrying of mails by any other than the government postal system, and Spooner's independent mail companies were virtually eliminated in 1845.

Spooner published other pamphlets, and in 1861, proposed a decentralized banking system similar to Greene's. It held that currency should represent an invested dollar rather than a gold or silver one, and that mortgages on fixed property should be the backing of money. Mortgages for redemption were always to be ample and open to public inspection.

Those who used the currency should know by what and by whom it was backed. In this way, a democratic, sound, and abundant currency with a low interest rate would be guaranteed by competition, limited only by the amount of real property, which was more plentiful than gold and silver.

Spooner introduced his bank project in 1864, and again in 1873, but did not succeed in getting it past banking and governmental opposition. His insistence that Congressional power "to coin and regulate money" did not include the power to make its use mandatory, and that debtors were free to pay debts in wheat, corn, hay, iron, wool, cotton, beef, or anything they choose, opened up ideas to be implemented later by others.

Through a long series of political writings, Lysander Spooner went on to unalloyed anti-statism. Through these run the concepts of natural law, natural justice, and natural rights, which led him to denounce all man-made government as superfluous. In *Constitution of No Authority*, Spooner questioned the validity of the U.S. Constitution itself. He held that signers of the U.S. Constitution had no power to contract for others than themselves in any matter. To maintain that a group of men might make political agreement binding on future generations was no more valid than to believe that they had power to make business or marriage contracts mandatory on future persons. Constitutional signers could pledge their support no longer than their own life span. The Constitution was the work of, and pledged the support of, only those who signed it.

In *Trial by Jury*, Spooner showed his distrust of government. He recommended that judges presiding over jury trials be elected by the people, and not appointed by government officials. From Spooner also comes the choosing of jurors from the names in a box.

In *No Treason* (1876), Spooner attacked the conduct of the Civil War, the Republican Party, and the whole structure of political democracy. He held that treason was conduct contrary to what had been pledged. Open revolt could not be treason unless prior consent could be proved. He contended that neither voting nor payment of taxes were valid evidence of either support or attachment to the Constitution.

Spooner's death in 1887 ended his pamphleteering.

Benjamin R. Tucker, Editor (1854–1939)

It remained for Benjamin R. Tucker and his journal, Liberty, to bring individualist anarchism into the Twentieth Century. Born in New Bedford, Massachusetts, the son of radical Unitarians in comfortable circumstances, he attended a local Friends Academy. He spent three years in Massachusetts Institute of Technology. Tucker became a supporter of Prohibition, women's suffrage, the eight-hour day, and of religious radicalism. Still too young to vote, he formed a political discussion club in New Bedford. In 1872, he met Josiah Warren and William B. Greene, and began a life-long career as an anti-statist thinker. Young Tucker's articles in The Word led to his association with its editor, Ezra Heywood. Through that journal, Tucker became familiar with Warren's labor exchange and "Cost, the Limit of Price"; with Greene's mutual bank, with J .K. Ingall's land occupancy-and-use; with Spooner's no-government, and with Heywood's literary productions.

Tucker became part of Heywood's staff on *The Word*, and in 1874, made the first of several trips to Europe to study the French anarchist, Proudhon. On August 8, 1875, Tucker announced his refusal to pay the poll tax in Princeton, Massachusetts, the home of Heywood. He was jailed, but soon released when an unknown friend paid his tax. Besides his long period of literary attack, this was Tucker's only clash with the machinery of the state.

Of more importance was the publication of Tucker's translation of Proudhon's 500-page *What Is Property?* For Tucker, Proudhon was the "profoundest political philosopher who ever lived." At age 21, Tucker was acknowledged a literary power, among America's outstanding voluntarists, all older than he.

Because Heywood gave too much space in the *Word* to "love reform rather than labor reform," and wanting to further explore economic justice, Tucker resigned to start his own radical review. On August 6, 1881, Tucker's first issue of *Liberty* appeared, saying:

> This journal will be edited to suit its editor. He hopes what suits
> him will suit his readers, but if not, it will make no difference.

DECENTRALISM

> *Liberty* is published for the very definite purpose of spreading
> certain ideas, and no claim to freedom of speech will be admit-
> ted to waste its limited space in hindering the attainment of
> that object.

With articles and discussion by Andrews, Spooner, Greene, Heywood and Ingalls, *Liberty* continued for 27 years, the longest-lived radical
periodical of economic and political nature in the nation's history, and
certainly one of the most interesting. Tucker was sure that "political and
social structures of American culture could be better dealt with after economic problems were settled. To be effective, *Liberty* must find its first application in the realm of economics."

Typical of Tucker's statements:

> Somebody gets the surplus wealth that laborers produce, and
> do not themselves consume…This somebody is the 'usurer'.
> Three forms of usury include interest on money, rent on land
> and homes, and profit in exchange…Free competition in a
> non-monopolized world tends to erase all three.

A typical editorial on "The Whole Loaf":

> The whole loaf rightfully belongs to those who raise the wheat
> from the soil, grind it into flour, and bake it into bread. Not the
> smallest taste of it to the sharpers who deceive the unthinking
> masses into granting them a monopoly of the opportunities of
> performing the operations, which opportunities they in turn
> rent back to the people, on condition of receiving the other half
> of the loaf.
>
> A monopolist is any person, corporation, or institution
> whose right to engage in any given pursuit of life is secured
> wholly or in part by any agency whatsoever against the influ-
> ence of competition.

Another salient discussion for which Tucker is remembered is his
comparison of Joseph Proudhon and Karl Marx, which he summarized:

The vital difference between Proudhon and Marx is in the respective remedies which they proposed. Marx would nationalize the productive and distributive forces. Proudhon would individualize them. Marx would make the landless political masters. Proudhon would abolish political mastery entirely.

Marx would abolish usury by having the state lay violent hands on all industry and business, and conduct it on the cost principle. Proudhon would abolish usury by disconnecting the state entirely from industry and business, and by forming a system of free banks which would furnish credit at cost to every deserving and industrious person, and thus place the means of production within the reach of all.

Marx believed in compulsory majority rule. Proudhon did not believe that 'numbers made a thing right'; he believed in the voluntary principle.

Tucker also compared State Socialism and Anarchism, showing "How Far They Agree And Wherein They Differ." This vindicated the Haymarket anarchists from violence and "revolutionary" intentions. Tucker never lost his conviction that the men were innocent, though he regretted their incendiary language which aroused the "statists" to act with malice and the death penalty.

4
henry george:
eliminating land monopoly

he life and work of Henry George in the last half of the 1800s was in the framework of decentralization in the United States and the world. He was born in 1839 in Philadelphia. As a child, he noted the squalor and misery of people in his neighborhood, alongside great wealth and riches. When he was fourteen years old, he left school to work in a store, and two years later, he sailed to Australia as a cabin boy. Everywhere the ship docked he saw this contrast between wealth and poverty—in the Mediterranean ports, in Egypt, India, China, and the South Seas.

Henry George wondered whether such conditions existed in the American West, newly opened to White settlement, where people were washing gold from running streams. He went to California to investigate. There too was destitution among beautiful buildings and spacious homes. Poverty *amidst* progress was the enigma of modern times. Why was this? He resolved to discover the reasons, and a solution.

As a printer, reporter, and finally editor of West Coast newspapers, Henry George pondered and reported on the disparity of wealth among people. One day, at the edge of San Francisco, he looked for a bit of land on which to build a home for his family. In an open area, with no houses in sight, he asked a man the cost of an acre there. "One thousand dollars," the man answered. "A thousand dollars for mere space—a vacant acre on which no work had been done! I work for a low wage," George remonstrated. "Why should I give my earnings and my labor to a holder of land who has done no work at all?"

George found in this incident a clue to poverty in the midst of plenty. Workers had to pay non-workers for space to live. He editorialized on this, and waged a vigorous campaign against government grants of land to railways. The railroad companies bought a controlling interest in his newspaper, and forced him out. The extraordinary rise in California land values at the completion of the railway ·confirmed George's contention that poverty was related to, indeed caused by, modern industrial progress.

In 1871, in a pamphlet, *Our Land and Land Policy*, George set forth the disadvantages of land monopoly—the holding of land by a few—and its effect on the condition and wages of the poor. He also won qualified approval of John Stuart Mill through an essay published in the *New York Tribune*. By 1879, George's full thesis appeared as *Progress and Poverty*. With pervasive logic, George showed the relationship and effects of the private ownership, sale, and rental of land.

1. He reminded readers that land is uneven in fertility and quality. On good land, a given amount of labor will produce much; on other land, the same labor will produce less; and on still other land, equal labor will produce little—or in some cases—nothing.

2. George stressed the ethical challenge in this situation: who should have the best, the good, and the poor land? Obviously, those on the best and good land have a natural advantage not shared by those on poor land.

3. When all land is free (as it was for "settlers" who had displaced the native nations), those acquiring land will take the best first. And most people will take more than they need—holding some for "the future." To hold land idle without using it, George pointed out, is to "withhold" it from others who need it.

4. Where people congregate, the value of land rises. Land value will be highest where most people live—usually in the center of cities; less at the edge; still less in remote and agricultural areas.

5. Thus, Henry George noted land, in addition to difference in fertility value, acquires a difference in site value, or location value. The site-value of land goes up in proportion to the industry and jobs available

near it. In the same way, land site-value increases as public services are made available to the residents on it, e.g., as churches, schools, libraries, streets, public services, and utilities are at hand.

6. Henry George traced the effects of rent on the general wage level. Rent is the difference between the production on the best land in use, and the production on the poorest land in use.

In *Progress and Poverty*, Henry George elaborated this process, and proposed a solution. Since public services largely create the value in land, Henry George proposed a double-pronged solution: let the local government collect the rent of land to pay for all public services, and at the same time, remove all taxation from labor products, improvements (buildings, equipment, etc.), sales and income. To collect land values for community use, and to remove taxes from buildings, would benefit farmers and homeowners, whose values in buildings, equipment, and capital are usually higher than in land values. It would encourage the use of land, instead of holding it idle. The use of land would move up to that yielding more than subsistence, and thus raise the general wage level for everybody. Access to land would be without purchase price. Shortly poverty would be eliminated; liberty and freedom would be advanced.

Henry George wrote, published, and campaigned valiantly in England, Ireland, Australia, New Zealand, as well as the United States. Favored by Labor, he was candidate for mayor of New York City in 1886. He was defeated, it was reported, by Tammany Hall.

In those times, Henry George was probably the most famous thinker and writer in the United States. He was always the center of controversy. Catholic prelates thought his teachings so contrary to established doctrine that in 1887, they ex-communicated Father Edward McGlynn because of his active support of George's ideas. The Holy Office ruled in 1889 that *Progress And Poverty* was "worthy of condemnation," which meant that bishops could forbid its reading to Catholics in their jurisdiction. Pope Leo XIII wrote "On The Condition Of Labor," directed against land reformers. In response, George wrote a long monograph, "The Condition of Labor: An Open Letter To The Pope," so lucid an explanation of the relation of land monopoly to poverty that one Catholic bishop said, "Next to the Bible, Henry George's writings lay claim to my devotion for expressing laws of love and justice." In a rare turn-around, the Church reinstated Father McGlynn in his parish.

A severe economic depression aided the reception of George's book, and by 1890, *Progress and Poverty* became the most popular book on economics published to that date. George presented an alternative both to Soviet Communism and to Finance Capitalism. George differed from both Adam Smith and Karl Marx. Adam Smith would individualize rent, wages, and interest. All three would go into private, individual, and corporate hands, i.e., Classical Capitalism. Karl Marx would socialize rent of land, wages and interest; all three would go into the hands of the state, i.e., Communism.

Henry George would socialize only the rent of land, i.e., its fertility and its site-value. Use-title to land would remain in the users' hands, as would wages and interest. But wages and interest would result from free action in a free market. Only rent of land would be used by the local community or local government, with all taxes removed from improvements, buildings, and labor products.

Henry George also wrote *Social Problems* (1883), *Protection Or Free Trade* (1885), *A Perplexed Philosopher* (1892), and *The Science of Political Economy* (1898). But it was *Progress and Poverty* which placed him in the front ranks of radical thinkers, and won many enthusiastic followers, including Leo Tolstoy. *Progress and Poverty* was elected to the Classics Book Club; it has been used as a university text in logic, so clear is its development from premise to conclusion. John Dewey said, "One can count on the fingers of two hands those who rank with Plato, and Henry George would be among them." *Progress and Poverty* has been translated into thirteen languages. It was estimated that in the quarter century before 1905, more than two million copies were sold, a larger market than the most popular novels of the day.

In 1897, Henry George was for the second time Labor's candidate for mayor of New York. Four days before the election, he died. His funeral in New York City brought such an outpouring of mourners that it is said to be the largest tribute ever paid a private citizen in the United States. The numbers of people, and the entourage, equalled that of the funeral for President U.S. Grant. On his gravestone were engraved his words:

> Acceptance of the truth I have taught will not come quickly. If that were true, it would have been accepted long ago. But the voice of truth is mighty, and it will come. One day, justice and peace will flood the world, and people will treat land as their common heritage.

The land monopoly is not the only monopoly, but it is the mother of all monopolies. Where George's proposals have been even partially accepted, land sites have become more accessible, business improved, and market-exchange freer. Denmark has changed her tax system in this direction under the leadership of the Justice Party, committed to land-value taxation. With it and thousands of cooperatives, Danish citizens have transformed their country into a flourishing beautiful countryside, supporting a large population in health and comfort. Melbourne, Australia, and sections of New Zealand, have flourished under land-value taxation.

Pittsburgh and Scranton, Pennsylvania, have long shown the benefits of a higher tax-rate on land than on improvements, and other cities are moving into this pattern. Southfield, Michigan, near Detroit, became a city of beautiful homes because of reduced taxes on buildings when taxation shifted to site-value of land.

Henry George was pre-eminently a decentralist. Collecting social values of land reduces and would eventually eliminate the monopolies that manipulate profit, wages, and interest. Removing taxes from labor products would insure workers a larger share of the products and wages they produce.

5
the cooperatives:
people uniting to own, control,
and operate their business

In 1844, twenty-eight struggling weavers in Rochdale, England, established the first cooperative store, using the principles now known throughout the world by their name, Rochdale, chief of which is distributing earnings to members in proportion to their patronage. From the beginning, this group sold at regular market prices, and returned to each member from the gross profits in proportion to the amount of that person's purchases in the year. This proved to be key to their growth, and in returning ownership, control, and direction to people generally in production, marketing, and credit enterprises.

The original capital of the Rochdale weavers was only 28 British pounds, for which each member had saved at two-pence a week. A hundred years later, 1944, the Rochdale Society of Equitable Pioneers had 90,000 members, and was the largest merchandising business in London. Their method has spread around the world, with outstanding growth in the United States.

Four basic principles undergird Rochdale Cooperation: open membership, democratic control, limitation on capital returns, and payment of patronage refunds to member-customers. Any person needing a cooperative's services may become a member (regardless of race, religion, or wealth) by purchasing one or more shares. Each member has one, and only one, vote in all meetings regardless of the number of shares held.

Only a limited interest is paid on capital. The earnings of the business belong to member-customers, and is returned in patronage refunds. If net return above cost is 5%, each person receives a refund equal to 5% of the amount he spent at the cooperative that year. Thus cooperatives achieve non-profit operation.

Cooperatives in the United States vary widely. The Associated Press is a cooperative belonging to member newspapers. And a handful of farmers in an isolated area have a cooperative for burials. There is hardly a human need but a cooperative is trying to meet it for its members.

Most families at some time—such as when death or illness strikes, or when a home needs building, or a young person goes to college—needs a source of credit. Banks have been reluctant to make small loans on the personal notes of people with little security—those who need it the most. By pooling people's savings, the credit union makes it possible for the whole group to meet members' credit needs when it is urgent. The credit union is another form of cooperative.

There are tens of thousands of credit unions in the United States, with millions of members and billions in assets. Most U.S. and Canadian credit unions are members of Credit Union National Association. Through its World Extension Division, credit unions are being set up in developing countries around the world.

All insurance is essentially cooperative activity, pooling savings and sharing risks by a large number of persons. But all insurance companies are not organized along mutual or cooperative lines. Mutual insurance companies develop active control by policy holders; they keep operating costs low, and return to policy-holders sizable dividends or premium reductions. Mutual insurance companies put policy-holders' money to work in their members' interest. They meet the insurance needs of groups organized around a common interest, such as a farm organization, labor union, community cooperative, or credit union.

In 1962, some 1,800 rural farmers' mutual fire insurance companies enabled farmers to share fire losses among themselves. With 12 million policyholders, $4 billions of insurance in force, and some $400 millions in premium income.

Cooperative health plans were created mainly to provide a budget method of paying for medical care which fits the average family income. Members pay monthly dues to an association which they control, and receive agreed-upon medical services through a staff of doctors and nurses. Patronage refunds are not made, but plans are operated at cost. The pioneer plan was the cooperative hospital at Elk City, Oklahoma. By 1962, nearly five million persons were receiving health and hospital care on a prepaid basis from group practice/health plans sponsored by communities, cooperatives, labor unions and employer-employee associations.

Cooperative home ownership of lower- and middle-income families has grown rapidly. In 1962, 60,000 people lived in cooperatively-owned apartment houses in New York City. Most of them were member-owners of projects sponsored by labor unions in the garment industry, dating from 1926. Amalgamated Homes in the Bronx is commonly-owned by 1,400 families, also owning a cooperative shopping center, operating a credit union, and sponsoring forums and lectures.

By 1960, 50 of the cooperative stores in the United States had reached the million-dollar mark in annual business. These 50 cooperative supermarkets had more than 150,000 members, and were doing a combined annual business of nearly $100 million. To be successful, a consumer cooperative must have a volume of business in natural trade areas, large enough to do efficient cooperative wholesaling, and some processing. "Co-op"-labeled merchandise has achieved a good reputation for quality and informative labeling.

The Central Cooperative, Inc., Superior, Wisconsin, since 1917, is one of the four large wholesale cooperatives, dealing in consumer commodities and farm supplies on a large scale.

National Cooperatives, Inc., headquartered at Albert Lea, Minnesota, is owned by 18 regional cooperative wholesalers and manufacturers. It makes milking machines and water heaters and procures automobile supplies, hardware, and groceries for its member-groups.

Independent retailers also cooperate. As early as 1887, a group of New York druggists pooled their order for a barrel of Epsom salts. As the chain store began to endanger the independent merchant's position, more and more retailer-owner wholesale houses were established. In 1960, about 100,000 grocers, 80,000 druggists, and thousands of hardware dealers, bakers, furniture dealers, lumberyards and feed dealers were served by these cooperative wholesalers. Through joint purchasing, they give the independent business one of the advantages of the nationally-integrated chain.

In the late 1960s and 1970s, a surge of small food-buying cooperatives developed. In churches, colleges, neighborhoods—anywhere people came together—they organized for quantity buying of quality food. Revealing their "protest" to the food industry (now the largest in the world), they sometimes call themselves "food conspiracies." One directory of such groups in 1977 listed names and addresses of 2,100 food cooperatives in the United States.

The Connecticut Dairyman's Marketing Association was the earliest agricultural cooperative. In the 1870s, the Grange began cooperative rural stores, one still active in Cadmus, Kansas. In the 1890s, fruit growers' marketing cooperatives were organized on the Pacific Coast. Most of the present cooperative businesses were established during the agricultural depression following World War I. Almost all of the large regional and wholesale manufacturers and farm-supply cooperatives were founded in the 1920s, with the most rapid growth in the depressed 1930s.

Eighty-nine percent of the U.S. farms had no electricity in 1935. The Rural Electrification Act, passed by Congress that year, provided that any competent borrower willing to furnish service to all farmers of an area who desired it might apply for low-interest, long-term government loans. Nearly all the applications came from cooperatives. From 1935 to 1962, electrified farms increased from 11% to more than 95%. Cooperative electrical distribution rates were reduced, and in some places, cut in half for all rural consumers. Some cooperatives established their own generating plants. In 1962, a thousand rural electric cooperatives distributed electricity to more than 5 million members. Their annual payments for electric energy were close to $750 million.

Three national federations serve cooperatives in general. The Cooperative League of the USA, founded in1916 (and of which Jerry Vorhees, a

Congressman from California, was president for many years), includes cooperatives of all types—rural and urban, consumer and producer, supply and service. The League represents American cooperatives in the International Cooperative Alliance in London, which holds a world congress every three years. The American Institute of Cooperation is an educational agency for agricultural cooperatives. It works with land-grant colleges for developing study courses in agricultural cooperation, and holds an annual educational meeting on the operation of agricultural cooperatives. The National Council of Farmers' Cooperatives is a conference body composed of many agricultural marketing and supply cooperatives. It performs legal and legislative work in Washington, D.C., and promotes research and expanded markets for agricultural products.

Though the size of some groups jeopardize decentralist values achieved through smallness, few cooperatives have reached the magnitude of centralized corporations. Cooperators, for the most part, are aware of the pitfalls of great size, and in one-member/ one-vote plan, maintain decentralized control. In most cases, local cooperatives practice another decentralist principle, federation (instead of unification), when joining larger or regional groups. This maintains local autonomy in their operations.

Cooperation and cooperatives are decentralist tools, largely in the distribution and marketing aspects of economics. Two important areas by their nature lend themselves to cooperation and await the widespread transfer from private ownership and control to cooperation. These are 1) the use, owning, and transfer of land, and 2) the issuing, valuation, and circulation of money. Cooperative land tenure and cooperative banking are challenges to decentralists and the decentralist revolution

6

ꞃalph BORSOᴆꞮ:
ᴆecentꞃaꞁꞮst supꞃeme

alph Borsodi's concern was good living. His search was as wide, deep, and complex as life itself. He was both an idealist and a practical man, a philosopher and an activist. In Ralph Borsodi's life and work, one finds a synthesis and integration of the goals and means of other leaders whose thinking contributed to the decentralist framework. He did not always use their contributions exactly as they presented them. Borsodi was an "original"—he adapted, added to, or improvised upon, the plans and principles of his decentralist forebears. He was a pluralist—not a one-idea man. He drew from America's early anti-statist individualists; he made creative use of Henry George's land-value tax; he applied cooperation to areas as yet largely neglected by America's cooperatives. He did not personally know any prominent anarcho-individualists, and did not come into contact with books and writings on the subject until 1950. Everything he did carried a distinct Borsodi stamp.

Ralph Borsodi was born in New York City on December 20, 1886. He grew up in lower Manhattan and in Europe, where his mother, suffering terminal tuberculosis, had taken him to visit Hungarian relatives. When she died, he remained, returning to the United States four years later when his father remarried. He had a few years of private, and no public schooling. He learned informally in libraries and in his home.

His father, William Borsodi, was a publisher, chiefly of the economics of Henry George and his followers. As a teenage assistant, Ralph

Borsodi heard and joined in conversations with authors, writers, and journalists. When Borsodi was a child, Henry George was campaigning for mayor of New York City. Borsodi did not meet him personally, but when he was still young, he was deeply impressed by hearing the son of Leo Tolstoy explain and quote from Henry George:

> Land values and rent increase with civilization. Rent swallows up the whole gain of civilization, so that pauperism accompanies progress...To see human beings in the most abject, the most helpless, and hopeless condition, go not to the unfenced prairies, but to the great cities where the ownership of a little patch of ground is a fortune.

Convinced of his logic and morality, young Borsodi brought his soap box to Union Square and discussed George's principles with all corners. He joined the Single Tax Party, and as editor of *The Single Taxer*, he called for a school of economics to teach the fundamentals of production and distribution of wealth. About 1926, Oscar Geiger acted on this idea, and formed and developed the Henry George Schools. Among the friends of Henry George and developers of his ideas who were often in the Borsodi home were Bolton Hall and Fiske Warren. Borsodi absorbed Hall's *A Little Land And A Living*, and Warren's *Enclaves of Economic Rent*.

About 1910, in his mid-twenties, Ralph Borsodi went to Texas to manage several hundred acres of land for his father. What to do with bare land in the wide-open spaces of Texas? Local residents advised Borsodi to hold on to the tract: "People are sure to move from the East to Texas. When they do, your land will go up in price. You might even become a millionaire!"

Borsodi was troubled by this conflict with his principles, this unearned gain in speculative holding of land. To have time to consider his situation, he bought a small-town newspaper, in which he reported on local happenings and discussed the land problem. Soon, he sold his father's acres for a modest figure, leaving the ethics of landholding to a newcomer.

Back in New York City, Borsodi was more than ever aghast at the concrete and brick canyons, with buildings soaring a hundred stories into the air. A few blocks away, millions lived in ghettoes. Borsodi saw the connection. Every building, giant skyscraper, or shabby tenement, occupied space—a bit of land—the owners of which were growing rich by collecting unearned wealth in rent or selling price of that land. Millions were living on the low wages left after rent was paid. Borsodi determined to do something to change and improve those conditions.

First he developed his own business as advertising/marketing consultant to large firms. In 1911, he married Myrtle Mae Simpson, a Kansas farm girl who worked in the Borsodi publishing company. They rented a house in Flushing, Long Island, where two sons, William Jr., and Edward were born.

In spite of his urban "success," Ralph Borsodi was dissatisfied with their crowded neighborhood, the insecurity of a rented home, the daily monotonous treks into the city for business, the counseling of clients on budgets to increase the sale of material goods, the growing consumer society, the decay of family life, honest labor, and a tie with the Earth.

At home, worries increased. The children had constant coughs and colds; Myrtle Mae was always tired with a severe case of anemia. Borsodi was frequently ill. At a business lunch one day, his friend, Hereward Carrington, preferred to omit the steak and potatoes. "I'm not eating today—got a head cold developing," he told Borsodi.

"What's not eating got to do with a cold?" a surprised Borsodi asked. Borsodi gave careful attention to Carrington's reply—that body ailments result from faulty nutrition, from over-eating or wrong eating, ending in uneliminated poisons or toxins in the body cells. "A fast—a time of not eating—gives the body a chance to rest. It allows the body to get rid of poisons, and return to normal functioning," Carrington explained.

As Borsodi read the literature offered by Carrington, his family joined in changing their food habits. In 1918, under the startled gaze of the Borsodi youngsters, Myrtle Mae chucked all their white bread and packaged cereals into the garbage can.

On spring Sundays, the Borsodis would pack a lunch and spend the day in the countryside north of the city. As they roamed the woods, their longing grew for a life in the country. A search for a home began. In 1919, they found a run-down seven-acre property in Rockland County. In spite of his lack of experience, Borsodi repaired and remodeled it. They gardened, produced and preserved food, and were delighted at the reduction of cash needed for their food budget. Meanwhile, Borsodi began writing in trade journals on modern business practices.

In 1923, Borsodi collected his writings in a 300-page book, *National Advertising and Prosperity*. He approved advertising *informing*—but disapproved advertising *persuading*. Wholesalers, announcing their goods to retailers, was economic, efficient, and cost-reducing. But national-brand advertising caused merchants to stock more goods unnecessarily, and persuaded customers, for illogical reasons, to want national-brand goods. Colgate toothpaste would make one "desirable to the opposite sex," the ads would say. Or wearing Hart Schaffner & Marx clothes would mean "success in business." Kellogg's cereals would help one "be a winner in sports." This kind of advertising wrongly stimulated consumer wants, Borsodi said, and it raised costs to merchants. An alternative was thorough and widespread consumer education in the worth and quality of goods bought.

A summer evening in 1920 was pivotal in Borsodi's discoveries. Myrtle Mae displayed six cans of their garden tomatoes she had preserved that morning. Borsodi was enthusiastic, but ever the economist, he asked, "Does it pay?" To be sure, he ran a cost-analysis. He calculated Myrtle Mae's work time, the cost of materials she used, the fuel consumed, and the maintenance cost of the equipment. Comparing these costs with store prices, he discovered that one person working in a modern kitchen was able to produce canned goods at 20 to 30% less than store prices of mass-produced goods. How could this be?

Myrtle Mae had no distribution costs, Borsodi noted. No advertising, no transportation, no selling. In *The Distribution Age* (1926) and *Flight From The City* (1933), Borsodi questioned the celebrated miracles of mass-production, and stated his law of distribution: "As production costs go down in mass, centralized production, the distribution costs go up." Long hauls from source of materials to factory, and from factory to consumers, plus the storage, advertising, handling, and selling costs, were absorbing and out-running lowered production costs. The centralized mass-producing factory, especially of food, was a real villain in the modern economic morass.

In a few years, the Borsodis built on 16 wooded acres their new Dogwoods Homestead—a large three-sectioned rock home, outbuildings for chickens, two goats and a pig. Eventually, they built two more stone cottages by the Flagg rock method, ready for when their sons would marry and bring their brides to Dogwoods. This site became Borsodi's homestead laboratory, from which he wrote America's first full critique of modern industrialism, *This Ugly Civilization* in 1929.

"Ours is an ugly civilization," he began. "It is polluted, noisy, hectic, over-consuming natural re-sources, and murdering time (man's most precious possession) in order to produce more goods. It fails to provide a means of living in which people find enjoyment in, and meaning for, living."

Borsodi presented the modern homestead as an alternative and challenge to industrial factory-workers. He described and showed the implication of Dogwoods Homestead, where they produced from the ground up. They made organic compost by layering vegetable and animal waste, kitchen refuse, and good earth. They tilled the resulting humus, full of living bacteria, into their soil. They planted and harvested green beans, peas, corn, tomatoes, carrots, potatoes, squash and pumpkins. They cared for a small flock of chickens and their two goats. They pruned old grape vines, berry canes, aging apple and pear trees. They were rewarded with bushels of fruit, although not always of first grade. "It's better to find a worm now and then, than to spray with chemicals," Borsodi said.

He stressed modernity. They used and applied modern electricity and tools: power saws, drills and sanders, tillers in the garden, canners and an electric mill in the kitchen. A human and decentralist technology eliminated drudgery of home production, Borsodi said, and would thereby lessen the use of factory machines, the chief evil of industrialism.

Factories are of two kinds, observed Borsodi. One kind are essential factories which produce desirable goods which can only be made in factories—wire, pipe, sheet metal, for instance. Then there are non-essential factories which produce either undesirable goods (such as patent medicines or nuclear bombs) or desirable goods, such as food and clothing, but which could be better produced at home or in small-scale groups. By Borsodi's measure, more than half of modern factories are non-essential.

Borsodi thoroughly analyzed the effects of the factory on its products, its workers, and its customers. Then he turned to analyze types of persons—the average person; the small percentage who are energetic, ambitious, and quantity-minded; and that smaller percentage who are quality-minded. When the quality-minded are in leadership, there is a beautiful civilization, Borsodi said. When the "quantity and power-minded rule," there is a materialist, "riches and poverty" civilization. And when the "herd-minded" rule, there is no civilization at all—there is only barbarism.

Borsodi completed *This Ugly Civilization* describing the barriers to his type of good life—formidable economic, political, moral and religious barriers to a beautiful, organic, human civilization. Hundreds of readers, in person and in letters, expressed their yearning for creative country life. Dayton, Ohio, Social Agencies invited Borsodi to assist in developing Liberty Homesteads Community, and their overwhelming unemployment problem. In 1936, Ralph Borsodi and friends established a School of Living homestead, at the center of 40 acres near Suffern, New York. Through unique cooperation, the School and homestead-applicants built Bayard Lane intentional community's sixteen two-acre homesteads, encircling the School.

Homesteading families became members of Bayard Lane Community Homestead Association. By their contract they were given use-title to two acres, not by payment of a purchase price, but by payment of a small annual rental to their Association for their land-title.

For building materials, the School of Living arranged a Cooperative Loan Fund, at low, rebated interest-cost to member homesteading families. The School also arranged Building Guilds of carpenters, masons and finishers, to guide and assist in home construction.

These unique types of land-use, financing and home-building, along with other activities and projects for economic, social and political change are available in Borsodi's books.

7

ROÐALES at the school of Living

In that learning-packed year (1939–40) during which I assisted at the Suffern, New York, School of Living, we never knew what special event each day might bring. One 1940 spring morning, I answered a knock to greet two people, relatively unknown then, but who would later influence American decentralism more than almost anyone else in this century.

"I'm J.I. Rodale from Emmaus, Pennsylvania" the man said, "and this is my son Robert. I have an appointment with Mr. Borsodi."

While the two men talked, Robert helped Reece and Betty May feed their rabbits and chickens, across the drive. At the time, Rodale was editor of a *Journal of Lexicography*. But his growing concern in 1940 was agriculture, and America's declining health. About these, he and Borsodi exchanged views. Borsodi showed him the library, with books shelved under major problems of living. Rodale spent several hours with the Health Problem group and at lunch exclaimed, "For me, your library is a gold mine! Scores of books which I need. That one small book by Dr. G.T. Wrench, *Wheel of Health*, fantastic! All about the remarkable people in the Himalayas, the Hunzas! Sturdy at more than a hundred years of age, mostly because of their natural food grown in such good soil."

Delighted, Borsodi nodded, and joined in, "On a diet of apricots, wheat and goat milk, especially from their specially fertile soil. Of course, the exercise in producing that food helps give the Hunzas their remarkable record!"

"It's amazing!" Rodale enthused, "how they engineered the water from mountain glaciers across their terraced gardens."

There was other table talk. "These muffins, Mrs. Borsodi," Rodale said, "are excellent."

"Made from our own flour ground in our electric kitchen mill, which we'll show you soon."

"You eat from your own supplies, entirely?" he asked.

"Almost," Mrs. Borsodi went on. "The beans are from our garden, frozen and stored over winter. The carrots and apples in the salad are from our root cellars, and the ice cream is from Nellie's milk, with our own honey added."

After lunch we toured the homestead, the gardens, the compost heaps, and stopped in the barn to pat Nellie and her new calf. Then Rodale went back to the library, to take notes, to marvel at Sir Albert Howard's *Living Soil and Agricultural Testament*, and F.H. King's report of the Chinese in *Farmers for Forty Centuries*.

"These are the things Americans need to know," J.I. Rodale said in 1940. "These would stem degeneration and disease. With them Americans could build health and stamina. I want to help them do it. I must study, experiment and publish what I learn."

His search took him far into the chemistry of food and soil; into questioning the use of chemicalized commercial fertilizers; into the Soil Association in England; into the bio-dynamic agriculture of Ehrenfried Pfeiffer, recently come to America from Switzerland. He made plans for new publications.

In 1948, J.I. began a radical new approach to health in a monthly journal, *Prevention*. To prevent, rather than cure, disease cut across accepted and deep-rooted views of medicine and health. Yet the response was good. The skill, wisdom and persistence of the Rodales and a growing staff extended subscriptions and impact rapidly.

Six years later (1953), Rodale issued *Organic Gardening* as a companion monthly to elaborate on the theory and practice of organic gardening. Very early, they published Ralph Borsodi's research, including the School of Living's experiment discovering the lower cost of preparing organic compost, as against purchasing chemicalized fertilizers. People's interest in, and their questions about how to garden organically, what to do and where, continued. While those first journals were 12 pages, 8 ½ x 11, today Rodale's journals are generously illustrated 200 pages of helpful articles and relevant ads, with a million subscribers and three or four times that many readers.

As the years went by, Rodale expanded their coverage to many aspects of homesteading: building, repairs, equipment, philosophy, reports, book reviews, questions and answers. A typical issue might have articles on Food Storage, Stocking up for Winter, Canning it Right, Building a Low-Cost Dryer, Using a Home Freezer. They even included social and cultural implications of decentralization. The Rodale journals are an on-going part of the decentralist revolution in America. They led (and lead) the way to a flow of books that practically saturate America in the 1980s.

8
the green revolution christened

In 1940, a growing group of persons concerned with the quality of life, rather than the overriding desire for things, were becoming interested in Decentralization. In the School of Living circle, more and more persons found their lives becoming integrated. In homesteading, they could be honest, practice social justice, experience personal growth, and live in harmony with nature. This trend received a name in a dramatic meeting at the School of Living.

In that year, School of Living forums were well received by progressives and radicals in New York City. Persons came as leaders and students from various groups. World War II had begun and serious people probed deeply. A particularly thoughtful group at the Education Seminar in January, 1940, included Dr. Stringfellow Barr, president of St. John's College of Annapolis; Morgan Harris, educational director of a major cooperative in New York City; William W. Newcomb, Georgist editor; Graham Carey, noted sculptor; Peter Maurin from *The Catholic Worker*, plus several teachers, homesteaders, and the School of Living staff.

Seminar members outlined their primary concerns and solutions for social ills. Graham Carey mentioned his debt to English distributists. Hilaire Belloc and Eric Gill, showed how art and responsibility are joined —both result from human work. A man tending a machine which makes boxes uses very little of his capacities. A craftsman carving a wooden bowl, on the other hand, uses his whole self—mind, body, will and feeling. He is therefore fully responsible for the object he makes. According to Graham Carey, then, a reform in work is the principal need of modern industrialism.

"No. The land problem is the first needing solution," maintained Bill Newcomb. He outlined the thesis of Henry George, and showed its relation to the on-to-the-land homesteaders. "Homesteaders are blocked by the high price of land. And nations go to war for profit in land and minerals. Land monopoly causes depressions and unemployment. Family security and world peace depend on ready access to land," declared Bill. "We've got to solve the land problem first."

"I maintain that cooperation is the first need for a better world," Morgan Harris offered. "Competition is our ruination; cooperation is an alternative." He showed how consumer cooperative groups eliminated middle-men. "If we don't cooperate, we will never solve world problems," Morgan declared.

Dr. Barr described the Great Books Program at St. John's University as a way to define and probe universal problems, and develop motivation and skill in solving them.

Mrs. Borsodi said, "I think the world's first need is good communication to help us reach agreement easily. That takes psychological insight and emotional maturing."

"And much adult immaturity comes from faulty child training," put in a teacher. "In my view nothing outweighs the loving, free relationships between adults and children, that children may have freedom to experiment and grow at their own pace and initiative."

Ralph Borsodi spoke. "You all have touched immensely important problems. You have demonstrated the complexity of education for living. Our need is for agreement on what constitutes universal, *major*, problems of living—the underlying and important ones—and of implementing human solutions for them. The School of Living attempts this. We see Graham Carey dealing with Occupation—work and leisure; Bill Newcomb with the Possessional Problem—who shall own land, goods, and other wealth. Morgan Harris sees the importance of How To Organize Enterprises. Of course, communication, child-parent relations, and Great Books are important. Let's develop an education which includes and integrates all."

Then he read the charter of The School of Living:

Believing that the full development of each human being is of supreme value, the School of Living has as its primary purpose to assist adults in their study and use of the accumulated wisdom of mankind.

Believing that wisdom is best forthcoming from the universal and perpetual experience of human beings, the School of Living aims to assist adults in becoming aware of, and in defining and dealing with, major problems of living common to all people, everywhere.

We sat by the fire, late into the night, seeking common ground. In the morning, Bill Newcomb summarized: "Each of us has a special axe to grind, a special reform to sponsor for that better world. Our professions and our work represent what is most important to us. Here at the School of Living, we've had a new concept of a good life, and an education for a good society. We've seen a larger whole. Each of our specialties is necessary, but not adequate alone."

"Right," agreed Morgan. "The School of Living is a wheel, of which each of us is a spoke."

"Or an umbrella," added Graham Carey, "which covers us all."

"The School of Living's job is synthesis—integration," Bill continued. "The School should federate—not actually unite us. That confederation would be a new movement. It needs a name. What should it be?"

Suggestions came. "The School of Living Movement," "Decentralization." "The New Age."

A sturdy peasant-like friend stood up. "I'm Peter Maurin of *The Catholic Worker*, just over from France," he said. "This morning the paper says Nazi planes are bombing my country. Troops are pouring across the border. Refugees are stranded along the highways, in the area of my home, my friends, and my family." He stopped and we waited.

"My people love life and the land. In every country, there are those who do. The only hope I see for the world is in the spirit and works like School of Living. In France, we call it "The Green Revolution." For a while, no one spoke.

63

"Good," said one. "I agree," another said. "Me too," from a third. Several nodded. Consensus was reached, and at lunch, Morgan Harris raised his glass of carrot juice, proposing, "Long life to the Green Revolution!"

The term found acceptance. Some used it in *Free America*, in the *Christian Century*, the *Catholic Worker*, and of course, in School of Living's *Interpreter*. From that beginning in 1940, the "Green Revolution" was our term for the decentralized, organic culture we worked for. In 1963, it became the official title of the School of Living monthly. THE GREEN REVOLUTION was spread in strong type across the masthead, and continues there to this day.

Gradually, the term Green Revolution spread. We sent the paper far and wide, often to officials in the United States Department of Agriculture. We reported on family homesteads, organic agriculture, activities in small communities. We discussed freeing the land of price and speculation, cooperative credit, a stable exchange media, replacing government with voluntary action.

The *Catholic Worker*, in the 1960s, published a book by Peter Maurin entitled *The Green Revolution*, in which he wrote:

The only way to prevent a Red Revolution
   is to promote a Green Revolution.
The only way to keep people from looking up
   to Red Russia of the Twentieth Century
Is to help them look up to Green Ireland
of the Seventh Century.

Imbedded here is not only the title, "The Green Revolution," but a philosophy of which Peter Maurin and Ralph Borsodi were leading spokesmen and demonstrators from 1940 onward. Definitely the term, "Green Revolution," meaning a decentralized society, was introduced to America from France, by the School of Living and the Catholic Worker in 1940.

9
school of living, global aspects

I n 1940, several factors necessitated the Borsodi's relinquishing active direction of the School of Living program. Mrs. Borsodi discovered active cancer, and for this they needed time for a demanding therapy of fresh vegetable/fruit juices, and travel to Dr. Edmond Sekley's health spa in Baja California, Mexico. At the same time, World War II upset the general economy, and financial support of the school dropped off. While a new staff administered the School, the Borsodis retired to Dogwoods to write and travel.

In 1941, Ralph and Lila Templin, and Paul and Betty Keene, were student-apprentices at the School. Both men had been Methodist missionaries in India, and assisted Gandhian forces in their crusade for independence from Britain. For this, the Methodist Board dismissed them from their posts. Returned to their homeland, they decided that the School of Living was "the closest thing to Gandhi in America." They visited, stayed on, and were glad to take over supervision and direction of the School while the Borsodis rested and traveled.

The Templins and Keenes began at once a full program of self-sufficiency: living frugally, planting and producing, and inviting students to share the program at a small fee. They improved the School's relations with the community homesteaders and extended cooperative activities during the troubled World War II years. Convinced pacifists, the Templins saw decentralization as a non-violent social pattern, consistent with their values. They presented decentralization to the peace movement. They organized a correspondence course of School of Living tenets, and community building. It was studied by men in Civilian Public Service

Camps, and in prison for conscientious objection to war. A crescendo was reached at the 1944 conference of the Fellowship of Reconciliation at Lakeside, Ohio, when Paul Keene emphasized self-education and self-development via communities and Schools of Living as non-violent ways to transform people and society. Among those affected, who became future decentralist leaders, were Robert Swann, co-founder of Community for Non-Violent Action, and International Institute of Independence, editor George Yamada, and Sonnewald Homesteader H.R. Lefever.

Responding to the world crisis, the Templins encouraged Ralph Borsodi in 1944 to write and publish his unique global peace plan. In it, Borsodi declared that 'nation' was an outmoded concept—an immoral, coercive institution. Borsodi showed that current plans to develop a League of United Nations, or a World Federation of Nations, is a mistaken direction. Rather, nations should relinquish their sovereignty, and in their place develop local communities and regions, along with three new world entities, based in ethical, decentralist concepts.

1. The first would be that ores, minerals, oils and fuels are the gifts of Nature to *all* humankind. From them, *all* people—not individuals, rulers, or corporations—should benefit. Rather than treat such mineral resources as commodities for profit and sale, Borsodi advocated a basic principle of Henry George's for global collection of their economic rent. To implement this concept, the first global entity would be a World Authority. The Authority would be restricted to one function—it is not a world government with over-all legislative, administrative, and judicial powers. A World Authority would only collect the land-site value, or economic rent, of mineral, fuel, and oil resources, and would allocate that to a World Patrol Force.

2. A World Patrol Force is different from a military force, Borsodi said. A World Patrol Force would consist of voluntary members, selected by Civil Service examination, from all parts of the world. It would have one duty—to patrol the land and seas to locate and inactivate any armament installations. It would encircle such armament facility—factory, ship, or troops—and prevent movement into or out of such facility. Financial support of a World Patrol Force would be the economic rent-fund of the World Authority.

3. Violators—producers of armament—would be reported to a World Court empowered to deliver judgment against such individual, corporate, or government violator.

Thus world peace would be obtained and insured, by effectively denying the profit incentive in dealing with world minerals, through channeling the economic-rent of minerals, fuels, and oils to the benefit of mankind, a new type of world authority, and world patrol. These would correct three fatal flaws in current world organization for peace, Borsodi said. It would eliminate nations; it would remove the primary cause for world conflict—the struggle for mineral and oil deposits; and it would give the World Authority an arm—the World Patrol Force—sufficiently coercive, but not violent, to prevent the making and use of armaments. Without armaments, there could be no war.

Ralph Templin further extended a hearing for decentralization in his doctoral thesis from Columbia University. In it, 1942, he described the School of Living and its program as an alternative, all-life approach to American adult education. After their term at the School of Living, the Templins worked with Dr. Arthur Morgan in Community Service, Inc., for the development of small communities. Templins built Glen Homestead in the Vale at Yellow Springs, Ohio. He taught sociology at Wilberforce University, and edited its *Journal of Human Relations.*

Robert and Agnes Toms, also former student-apprentices at the School of Living, followed the Templins as directors. They ably managed the School's program, but difficulty arose in a conflict around the community-tenure of land. The by-laws of Bayard Lane Association restricted the use of land to family homesteading; it prohibited commercial enterprises. One homesteader, Hugh Merrell, envisioned his successful homestead chicken flock being extended to 1,000 layers, and the selling of eggs and broilers to hundreds of customers.

In leaning toward democracy, Ralph Borsodi had included in the by-laws a return to private ownership of land on a vote of three-fourths of the homesteaders. Restive and ambitious Hugh Merrell campaigned to change the land-tenure back to private ownership—to dissolve the community bond—in order to develop his chicken business. With skillful propaganda, he brought the issue to a vote. Again, as in Dayton, Borsodi's cherished experiment faced a decision on moral principles. Again, the vote was negative. The community land was returned to private property and ownership by sixteen separate families.

With the core of his program lost, with dwindling finances and an ailing wife, Borsodi agreed to the sale of the School of Living to Larry Wray for use as a family homestead. The School's library and the core of its program were transferred to the Loomis Lane's End Homestead in Ohio. Borsodi turned to publishing further interpretation of his ideas and experiments. He bought a linotype and on it set in hot metal, two volumes of *Education and Living*.

Completed in 1948, Volume I described and documented six over-riding kinds of centralizations: of distribution: land-rent in distributing wealth and long-hauls in distributing goods; of production: mass factories; of possessions: monopoly, and maldistribution of wealth; of government: increase of size and functions into federal units; of residence: large cities and megalopolis; of education: huge schools and colleges.

The second volume described his concept of normal individuals, normal families, normal communities, regions, and world—an outline for a decentralist revolution. He challenged teachers not to follow and pass on a centralized culture, but to lead in the development of Normal (optimal) Living. Ralph Templin said, "In *Education and Living*, Borsodi has outlined a program to keep people working for a thousand years."

Then the break came. Myrtle Mae died in 1948. Their natural foods and other regimens were not adequate. They felt that wrong-living habits in childhood and youth had so undermined her resistance as to be irreversible in her later years. Borsodi began to travel more frequently. He traveled to China, Thailand, and India to examine Eastern family and village cultures. He was disappointed, however, to find largely a copying of the industrialism of the West; his analysis and recommendations are in his *Challenge of Asia* (1956).

From his youth, and particularly since *This Ugly Civilization* in 1928, Borsodi had worked prodigiously for decentralization. Since the 1940s, he rejoiced at similar writing and projects in the same vein, from students and early associates. Remaining chapters report the activities of many of them. The first is Agnes Toms, and her influence in improved nutrition.

10

agnes toms and whole foods

Of the several facets of a Decentralist Revolution, one of the first to capture and hold the people's interest is a change in nutrition and diet. Good eating is not only a prime need for survival, but of gastronomic pleasure. It's a simple dictum that says, "You are what you eat." The further one gets into the miracle of soil becoming food, becoming flesh, blood and bones, the more fascinating the study becomes. It is fortunate that this is so, for the difficult process of changing habits—including food habits—needs all possible support.

By 1940, most Americans had fallen into a host of personal and social errors. In their faith in big cities, big industry and big government, the average American had become an unthinking and helpless victim of packaged, devitalized foods, and to big commercial agriculture back of it, with its depleted soil, chemicalized fertilizers and sprays, and wrong tilling. Junk and snack foods were everywhere, sometimes labeled "The Terrible Ten": white bread, doughnuts, coffee, sugar, packaged sweetened cereals, carbonated sugar drinks, potato chips, hot dogs, sweetened baby foods, and "smoked" meats.

The School of Living called for a halt to this modern trend. It set a standard with its program of composted soil, organic gardening, home-preparation and eating of natural whole foods, home-grinding of grain, home-baked bread, careful storing and preservation of fruits and vegetables. To most of the School's students, this was new and challenging.

So it was in 1942 to Agnes Toms, a graduate of the University of Southern California, with a master's degree in home economics from Columbia University in New York. All her training had been in the orthodox ideas and methods of teaching foods and nutrition. She had taught conventional home economics in California high schools for ten years. But a three-week seminar with Ralph Borsodi opened her eyes. Day after day, Borsodi's lectures, along with reading in the School's library, changed her concept of health from the older medical position to the new world of natural healing via food, nutrition, and agriculture.

Nine books in the School's library turned as many aspects of the older notion to a holistic approach to health. Each book and its author contributed to the history of Decentralization, and are still valid reading. Each deeply affected Agnes Toms, and through her, many others in today's revolution in food habits.

Nine Relevant Challenges to Conventional Nutrition
First in time and importance is a small book, Bread by Sylvester Graham, published in 1837. Simply and directly he told, a century ago, why food is best in its natural state:

> If people were to subsist wholly on substances in their natural state, or without any artificial preparation by cooking, then they would be obliged to use teeth freely in masticating, and in so doing, keep teeth in sound health. At the same time, they would thoroughly mix food with saliva, and thus prepare it for swallowing and for action for the stomach. People would swallow food slowly as the welfare of the stomach and the whole system requires they should.

Further, he points to deterioration in food caused by improper tillage of the soil. "I have no doubt it is true that the flour and wheat raised on a soil cultivated with a recently-applied crude, stable manure may readily be distinguished by its odor from the flour of wheat raised on a new and un-depraved soil, or from wheat raised on a soil dressed with *properly* digested manure." Sylvester Graham added: "If similar results of improper tillage can become sources of serious evil to the human family, through their effects on the flesh of animals which man devours, and on the milk and butter which he consumes, surely the immediate effect on vegetable matter on the same human system must be considerable."

Graham's recommendation is clear. "The best way is for every family to raise, or purchase, sufficient quantities of the best new wheat produced by proper tillage in good soil; put it away in clean casks, where it will be kept dry and perfectly sweet; and as they need it take one or two bushels, wash it thoroughly but briefly in two or three waters (wheat kernels must be free of dust, rust and smut) and spread it on sheets to dry for a day or two and then grind it as needed."

Then he explains how to make good bread of whole-grain flour. (The Lee Foundation for Nutritional Research of Milwaukee reprinted this significant century-old treatise in the 1950s.)

A second challenge came early in the 20th Century by authorities who proved that most body illness did not come from germs and bacteria, but was a systemic, body condition of malfunctioning cells, glands, and organs. *Toxemia Explained* by Dr. John Tilden explained that poisons and toxins in the body resulted from faulty or deficient nutrition, or by over-eating or wrong combination of foods.

Number three introduces the healthy Hunzas, that incredible tribe in northern India whose members live to be 100 or 200 years old with such excellent health that their old men carry burdens over crags and peaks for missionaries and explorers. The Hunzas engineered troughs to bring the glacial waters with mineral silt to flood their terraced gardens. Their fertile soil, healthy plants and animals resulted in human energy and stamina. A tribe in the same climate and topography did not "build" their soil, and were sickly, infertile, and degenerate.

Dr. G.T. Wrench, an English medical officer in India, was the first to bring knowledge of the Hunzas to the West. Dr. Wrench told their story to the American Medical Association in 1921, with little or no response. It was only as his book, *The Wheel of Health*, was published and a few copies were circulated by the School of Living, that it began to affect nutrition in modern America. Others who have visited and reported on the Hunzas are Allen Banik, Art Linkletter, and movie actress Renee Taylor, author of *Hunza, Himalaya, Shangrila*.

Preceding and following the interest in the Hunzas, there were writers who stressed the relation of humas-laden soil to well-balanced, healthy plants and healthy animals who ate the plants. F.H. King in 1902 developed this thesis in his book titled *Soil*. He described Chinese agriculture in 1935 in *Farmers For Forty Centuries*.

Sir Albert Howard of England and Dr. Weston Price, a Cleveland dentist, detailed how and why impoverished soil means plant, animal, and human disease. Soil depleted of organic humus loses its trace minerals, resulting in imperfect synthesizing of protein in the green leaf. Gradually, Nature's protection in the living cell is lost. Only by obeying Nature's law of return—the return of all vegetable, animal, and human wastes to the soil—will such conditions be reversed. High nitrogen, sulphurized, chemical fertilizers must be avoided.

Sir Albert Howard's *Agricultural Testament* and *Soil and Health* were published in the United States by Devin Adair Co. in 1947.

Dr. Weston Price's *Nutrition and Physical Degeneration* is the result of his world tour of countries where people lived on native, well-cared for soil. Hundreds of photographs in his 525-page book show that people living on native food from virgin soil had broad dental arches and superb health. This was true whether their diet consisted of goat milk and cheese in Switzerland, grains in Africa, rice in India, or fruit in South Sea Islands. Members of the same tribes who had turned from native diet to white sugar, white flour, and tinned meats of the West, had rampant tooth decay and narrowing dental arches.

Thus did nine revolutionary books challenge the traditional Nineteenth Century view of health and healing. One of the world's great scientists of this period was early in this framework. None other than Dr. Charles Darwin, compiler of the theory of evolution, wrote in 1820 *Humus and The Earthworm*, a fascinating account of the lowly creature that makes soil a living environment, not merely a chemically-inert one.

The valiant authors of these books stood in the path of Industrialism's juggernaut. Where their messages were heeded, the damage of agribusiness has been moderated. In spite of these books, however, moderns were swept into an energy-and-resources crisis of worldwide proportions. (Probably the most effective alert to the fragility of the earth and the emergency of sheer survival was Rachel Carson's *Silent Spring*, 1962. Revolutionaries of the 1960s found ammunition in her documented proof of harm from chemical fertilizers and over-population. Unless such trends were reversed, she said, a Spring would come where no more birds would sing.

In these seminal books, the basis for a revolution in food, nutrition, and agriculture was available in the School of Living library 1940-45. Practically everything written on health since the 1930s is an extension, elaboration, or example of the ideas and practices in those nine or ten books. Among the people who eagerly studied them at the School of Living were J.I. Rodale, Paul and Betty Keene, Agnes Toms and myself.

Agnes Toms was convinced of the wisdom and importance of the School's work. In 1940, she gladly took over management of the School's food program under the helpful guidance of the Borsodis.

For breakfast for from four to twenty students, Agnes Toms ground grains—wheat, oats, rye, buckwheat, barley—in the electric kitchen mill. A favorite cereal was whole-wheat kernels from a nearby farm, soaked over night and steamed for an hour the next day. With honey from the School's bees and cream from the cow, the cereals were delicious and nutritious.

Apples were always available. Homestead fruits were canned or frozen, chiefly blueberries, in great supply. Many fruits were dried in a dryer invented by Ralph Borsodi. Fertile eggs from chickens who scratched in the ground and ate live bugs, worms, and bacteria added to the nutrition. Mrs. Borsodi and Agnes Toms made or supervised making all the cottage cheese, butter, yogurt, and ice cream eaten there. Ham, bacon, and sausage were from the School's animals. Time-saving electrical equipment assisted: range, chopper, blender, grinder, refrigerator, freezer, and the cherished flour mill.

People said they had never tasted anything so good as the bread made each day from freshly-ground flour. Honey, molasses, and freshly-ground peanut butter were so good they had trouble keeping them on hand. For lunch, fruit, melons and berries—fresh in summer, frozen in winter—accompanied fresh bread, a hot vegetable soup, and a green salad.

73

They followed Borsodi's recommendation to increase vegetables and decrease meat consumption.

The evening meal was a gala affair, with people enjoying vegetables, a raw fruit salad, with chicken, duck, turkey, fish or a favorite bean and cheese casserole. Everyone helped prepare the popular biscuits, muffins and breads of whole-grain flour. Desserts were ice-cream, fruit cobblers or shortcakes of whole flour. They often lingered at the fireplace with fresh fruit or berries, cheese and coffee. Snacks at the School of Living in the mid-1940s were home-grown sunflower seeds, peanuts in the shell, popcorn and apples, or raisins and dates bought in bulk from California organic farms.

Robert and Agnes Toms returned to California in the late 40s, ever grateful for the Borsodi leadership and the School of Living library in those beginning years of the natural foods movement. Agnes again taught foods and nutrition, but this no longer included the use of refined, processed foods. She could not now recommend pasteurized milk, nor work with foods grown on chemically-treated soil or sprayed with poisons. She located sources of natural foods to supply the school.

But since there were no textbooks from the organic, natural point of view, she wrote her *Delicious and Nutritious*, the first natural foods cookbook ever published. From long use in the Monrovia Public Schools, it spread widely. Her students had projects to spread the word, such as one group which baked and distributed whole-grain bread at the Los Angeles County Fair.

Patterned after Dr. Pottenger's experiment with cats, one of Agnes Toms high school classes fed groups of mice different diets. One group had whole grains, cheese and fats; another had packaged, commercial cereals, pasteurized milk, and processed cheese. Students were amazed at the results. The whole-foods mice had large well-formed bodies, sleek hair, lively habits, and litters of several babies. Mice on packaged foods were small, scrawny, with body sores. They were alternately quarrelsome or listless, with small or no litters.

Newspapers began reporting Agnes Toms' exhibits and teaching methods. Soon, a large file bulged with clippings about "Natural Foods Being Taught in Public Classroom."

In 1948, she joined the American Academy of Applied Nutrition, a group of doctors, dentists, and other professionals seeking prevention of disease and dental caries. They were impressed by the books that had influenced her at the School of Living, particularly those of Dr. Weston Price, Sir Albert Howard, and Dr. F.M. Pottenger. She reviewed books, lectured, and demonstrated in the Academy's adult study groups. At conferences, she displayed her textbook, and others published by Devin Adair—*Eat Drink and Be Healthy* (1963) which was later paperbacked as *The Joy of Eating Natural Foods.*

Since 1960, Agnes Toms has provided monthly columns for *Modern Nutrition*, of the American Nutrition Society; *Natural Foods* of the Natural Food Associates; and *Let's Live*. In 1974, her second popular book was published, *Natural Food Meals and Menus for All Seasons*. Through Agnes Toms, Borsodi had a basic and notable effect on America's food.

Later Food and Nutrition Literature

Since the 1930s, authors and books on the nutritional approach to health began a continuing flood. Ruth Stout popularized her mulch/no-tilling method in Gardening Without An Aching Back and in Green Thumb Gardening. Past 80, she experiments and reports her results in health and gardening magazines.

Heading the list in sales and influence is Adelle Davis' popular trio: *Let's Eat Right, Let's Cook It Right, Let's Have Healthy Children. Reader's Digest* featured her; use of her "power foods" (wheat germ, yogurt, brewer's yeast) has become a badge for acceptance into the avant garde where Adelle's name is a household word.

Equally popular was Cathryn Elwood, who in *Feel Like A Million* dispensed scientific nutrition in a cheery lively manner. Both Cathryn and Adelle grew up on commercial foods. Both were sickly and under par until they learned good nutrition. Both had college degrees in nutritional research. When they began practicing what they preached, both achieved youthful vigor, each living until nearly eighty years of age.

Another writer is Beatrice Trum Hunter, whose titles include *Natural Foods*, *Gardening Without Poisons*, and *Consumer Beware!*

While food and family health have a predominance of women authors, scores of prominent men join them. Dr. Royal Lee of the Lee Foundation for Nutritional Research has reprinted millions of informative pamphlets. The School of Living's *Interpreter* quoted from and featured him as early as 1950.

Scores of groups have formed to educate on specific aspects of the developing controversy between natural and artificial foods. The Natural Food Associates of Atlanta, Texas, of which Dr. Joe Nichols was president for 25 years, emphasizes whole food from fertile soil. Their membership journal, films, and conferences influence hundreds of thousands of people. In 1975, they began developing an 800-acre demonstration farm near their headquarters. (Natural Food Associates was formed in 1951 through the efforts of several young farmers, including Alden Stahr of Layton, New Jersey, and Robert Rowe of Illinois. They published two volumes of *Normal Agriculture*, later to be titled *Natural Living*. Articles about Lane's End Homestead, Ralph Borsodi and Paul Keene appeared in their October, 1953, issue.)

The National Health Federation stresses freedom of choice in health matters. They constantly lobby against laws that restrict individuals in their learning about health, or in choosing their own method of healing, including non-traditional ones. Headed by Oscar Crecelius in California, and Clinton Miller in Washington, D.C., they champion freedom from medical monopoly. They question the right of any governmental authority to add fluorides to public water; they clarify attempts to classify vitamins as drugs or to impose restrictions on the sale of food supplements.

Dr. Herbert Shelton heads the Natural Hygienists (San Antonio, Texas). Hygienists hold that good health results only from living by six natural laws: eating natural foods, drinking pure water, breathing pure air, having adequate physical exercise, satisfying sex, thinking constructively, and feeling positively. Hygienists are developing a 1,600-acre homesteading community near their headquarters.

Young Jay Dinshah of Malaga, New Jersey, helps stage a world conference of vegetarians each summer. In 1975, more than a hundred leaders shared with 2,000 delegates from all parts of the globe in a wide spectrum of health education. In 1977, their world congress was in New Delhi, India.

Health Foods—A New Business

Now that health foods are in demand, they are available both on supermarket shelves and in special stores. Directories of bona fide health stores list thousands in all parts of the country. Production, distribution and sale of health foods claim the attention of business experts. Beginning in the 1930s with Deaf Smith County (Texas) wheat, it now includes busy Shiloh Farms in Oklahoma and Pennsylvania, and Erewhon Distributors in Boston. Nutrition firms tell millions of homemakers about natural foods in Family Circle and Women's Day. Bob Hoffman, York, Pennsylvania, businessman, and physical therapist, has seen his special protein foods find national acceptance through free distribution of an informative journal, World Health and Ecology News. Spontaneous food buying cooperatives, sometimes called food "conspiracies," number more than 2,000 in 1977.

A food reform is spreading and deepening, rooted in thinking undergirded by both science and philosophy. The American public has moved a long way in nutrition since the 1930s, signaling a revolution in culture. Agnes Toms and many others are grateful to the Borsodis for their part in it, and glad that Dr. Borsodi lived to see the surge of interest, after working for it sixty years until his death in October, 1977.

Not all are persuaded to natural foods. Housewives still wheel enormous carts of devitalized, packaged foods from supermarkets. The U.S. Food and Drug Administration (FDA) still bows to food processors, as evidenced by the following item repeated on many TV stations and in the press.

Four myths exist regarding food in the American public:

The myth that most diseases are the result of faulty diets. The fact is that very few diseases, in this country at least, stem from dietary deficiencies.

Myth No. 2 charges soil depletion with being the culprit in malnutrition. Soil composition has little appreciable effect on the composition of the plants grown on it. While it is true that certain soil elements are needed for *growth*, they do little to affect nutritional *quality*.

A third myth holds that commercially-processed and cooked foods lack nutritional value. These include canned food, refined cereal, white flour, and even pasteurized milk. The truth is that though some raw fruits and vegetables are desirable, modern processing techniques do not harm, but help produce foods with high nutritional value.

The last of the four myths contends that, because most of us suffer from 'subclinical deficiencies' (those with no observable symptoms) we need to supplement our diet with various vitamins and minerals. The truth? If you're in good health and eat a variety of foods, you don't have to fret about any deficiencies in your diet. Foods are the best nutrient sources. (Quoted from *Ground Water Age*.)

The books commented on at the beginning of this chapter, and the hundreds of testimonies in scores of health journals, prove that the FDA release does not refute what it calls myths. The continuing swing to natural foods, natural healing and natural agriculture is part of the Revolution for Decentralization.

11
walnut acres
chooses to stay small

The lives of Paul and Betty Keene were changed at the School of Living. In 1940, after a teaching stint in India, the Keenes spent a summer on the farm of a friend in the Catskill Mountains. They loved the soil and loved working in it. They found the School of Living in nearby Suffern, New York, where "intellectuals were doing things with their hands." They read the home production *How To Economize* bulletins, and were fascinated by the savings they made following them.

That fall, teaching math and physics at Drew University "didn't seem right." Paul's work on his doctoral thesis was distracted by visions of fertile fields, barns and animals, and tender growing things. Realizing they were marching to a different drummer, the Keenes knew they were destined for the country. In the spring of 1941, they became co-directors of the School of Living with the Templins.

"Our two years there," they say, "were rich and formative beyond all asking." The School's students and teachers were pioneering into the future. At its heart was the library with incredible ideas, many of whose time had come. And there to challenge, interpret, direct and expand stood the Borsodis—original thinkers, indefatigable doers, born teachers. For the Keenes, the homestead had come alive. They caught a glimpse of the oneness and wholeness of life.

Close by, in Spring Valley, New York, was Three-Fold Farm, its program based on the teachings of Rudolph Steiner in Germany. Fred and Al-ice Heckel had studied Biodynamic Farming there, and helped establish the methods in the School of Living program—companion planting, and compost heaps with special starter made from chamomile, stinging nettle, and other herbs, along with hormones from animal entrails.

The Keenes' work at the School of Living inspired them to make their complete living from organic farming. After two years at Kimberton Farm's Steiner School, they felt ready to go on their own. During their first year on rented land, they suffered the tragic loss of all their crops in July hail storms, which washed much of their soil into the Delaware River. They borrowed $5,000 to buy 100 acres of rolling land in Central Pennsylvania, with house, barn, and sheds. In March, 1946, Paul, Betty, their two children, Betty's father, a team of horses, a dog, ancient bits of furniture, and an old car moved to their own farm, Walnut Acres.

Early German settlers had looked for black walnut trees as indicators of the limestone soil they sought. In Penns Creek, Pennsylvania, their new farm was full of them, some standing, no doubt, when William Penn lay claim to all land thereabouts.

No mother ever looked more fondly on her new-born than Paul and Betty viewed Walnut Acres as they rattled proudly up the winding lane by the stream. Glory was everywhere. The tin roofs were rusted through in spots? Set buckets under the drips until there is time to patch the holes. Buildings haven't been painted in twenty years and windows falling out? Ah, but the wood is sound—just paste papers over the holes for now.

No plumbing, no bathroom, no telephone, no furnace—they must heat with wood? But isn't it great to pioneer? They must live and pay off the mortgage with one team of horses, an old plow and harrow? Well, they had lived on nothing before. Now they had a house and barns and a hundred acres!

The years went by. Soon there were three children and two teams of horses. Then the horses left and a tractor came. Always cows, sheep, chickens, guineas, ducks, geese, bees, rabbits, cats and dogs. How soon all grew together into one family, each knowing and accepting the other, albeit sometimes grudgingly.

Slowly, life returned to their soil. They built terraces, grassed water-ways, and contour-strips to control water run-off; they planted clover and alfalfa everywhere, and allowed heavy sods to grow. They chopped grasses and legumes back into the soil instead of making hay with all of them; they left all the straw on the ground after harvest; they fed the soil peanut hulls, corn stalks and hundreds of tons of ground rocks, manures, composted materials and industrial wastes. They took off fewer crops than most farmers, leaving each field to its own recuperative devices one year out of four.

In the early years, they had insects, but these diminished until now they find no more than one variety a year that may need special attention. Yields approximate those of their more chemicalized neighbors, but are less in total because of the fallow year allowed their fields. Over all, the Keenes and their farm have grown into a mutually helpful unit. In husbandive, non-exploitive partnership, they feel the satisfaction and the reverence which country folk have felt from time immemorial.

While the Keenes were falling in love with their Elysian fields, they were aware of a growing interest in them from the outside. First in ones and twos, then in growing numbers, people wrote, or came to see them at work. Visitors wondered if they might buy foodstuffs raised without chemicals or poisonous sprays. The Keene's process made such elemental sense that people were willing to pay extra costs of maintaining a healthy soil for its balanced, tasteful products.

Their first sale crop was apple butter—Apple Essence, 500 quarts the first year. They'd spend whole days in the sun and wind, stirring the bubbling apple pieces in cider in a big black kettle, over a roaring woodfire. Daddy Morgan spelled them off, infant on one arm, stirrer in the other hand.

Soon they shipped out carrots, potatoes and onions by parcel post. Then dressed chickens, eggs in metal containers, honey from their bees, blankets made from wool sheared from their own sheep. Once they crated a live lamb and sent it off. Next, a small hand-mill with which they laboriously ground whole-grain flour and cereal. Later, an electric stone-burr mill and other refinements, including a walk-in refrigerated storage room for perishable grains and flour.

All the time they remodeled chicken house, horse stable, the big barn with added on portions, until now a nice variety houses their milling, storage, and merchandising of whole foods. Faithful, understanding and friendly customers now number tens of thousands. Some come to the Walnut Acres farm store; others order by mail

The Keenes were one of the first to enter the natural foods business. Their name is now well-known in America and in some places abroad. They did not plan this—originally they just wanted to get away from that infertile crescent stretching from Boston to Richmond, to live simply and quietly, raising their family in a typical, conservative rural society. But they found themselves caught up in a wider movement. They would have felt remiss not to have given it the best they had.

Now there are seventy friends and neighbors working together, generally in unity and fellowship, producing a great variety of quality foods. On the farm, now 500 acres, is an enlarged farm kitchen and storehouse. They grow, harvest, store, grind, bake, roast, toast, combine, can, freeze, package and ship literally hundreds of good foods. Whole foods from properly prepared soil are prepared in small, labor-intensive batches, daily or weekly. Perishable foods are sent the day the orders arrive—no storage in jobbers' warehouses or on grocers' shelves. At no time are any of the thousands of commonly-used synthetics or artificials introduced. Every ingredient is listed on each label. In every case for every purpose, from seed to consumer, the Keenes have sought the best.

Thousands of letters come, telling what better, whole foods have meant to individuals and families. Occasionally, second-generation Walnut Acres fed children have visited, and the Keenes are cheered by their bloom, awareness and alertness. A great responsibility, a tremendous possibility, and a rare and heart-warming privilege it is to see the results of one's effort in living human beings.

Walnut Acres is not organized into a special community. As individuals and families, they live separately from one another in the rural community of Penns Creek. Walnut Acres does not depend on special living conditions or philosophical leanings. Its approach to business affairs could succeed anywhere.

A person, after happily working with Keenes for two years, becomes eligible for membership in Walnut Acres, Incorporated. Five shares of stock are given to each member annually for twenty years, for a maximum of 100 shares. The corporation owns the whole enterprise, land, buildings, equipment, inventory, supplies, formulae, and mailing list.

The worker–stockholders own the business, and share in its risks and successes. The former seem to outweigh the latter, but at the heart of the daily work is a rightness and fairness which makes for genuine happiness and satisfaction. They say, "It is *our* venture, *our* business. Together we feed thousands with the best of foods. Our purpose ties us and the universe into a meaningful whole, in which soil and people cooperate. We help less-fortunate people, locally and far afield, through our small Walnut Acres foundation."

The Keenes have wondered sometimes about their growth. They have not wanted to be so large they couldn't apply their ideals to all parts of the work. They feel they are close to the ideal size, allowing the genuine involvement of all in every aspect. Over the years, they have fought off growth for growth's sake. Each move, each replacing of hay in the barn loft with piled-up cartons of canned foods, wrenched their spirits. They took each step always for what seemed valid reasons.

In the 1970s, people everywhere awoke to an energy crisis—to the fact that all are earthbound creatures, "that we live fully only as we keep wholesome, reciprocal contact with the soil." National food manufacturers and chain stores are never slow to sense a bandwagon, nor reluctant to jump on. It wasn't long until they began dashing about, seeking supplies of "natural foods."

The Keenes were approached from all directions with million dollar offers to sell out, with inquiries about expanding enormously with their additional capital; with appeals to manufacture and sell their food through larger companies. These offers were fun for a while, but not in the least tempting. The Keenes simply did not consider upsetting the philosophy and the practice of a lifetime for mere money. They felt some-what self-righteous during that period—their size felt so good.

Basically, they still think small. They live one day at a time, plant one field at a time, harvest one crop at a time. They've adopted a decentralist or intermediate technology, using slower machines of earlier years. People are at the center. Fields are small, averaging three acres; their village is small, with 400 residents; their church, school, neighborhood groups are small. They have found richness of life in smallness.

Walnut Acres is simply a good living on the land. Around them are frugal Amish families on good farms of one or two hundred acres. Through careful planning, hard work and simple living, the families carry on happily. Because of hills, stones, and small fields, farming there is different from that of Iowa; topsoil is not deep, and yields may be less. In the 1970s, an Iowa agribusiness farmer needs a million dollars to buy land, buildings, and equipment to start farming. How they push the soil to get that back! Even near Walnut Acres, land is high-priced enough so that a young person, without family help, cannot take up farming. When consumer prices are set so that Iowa farmers just make a decent living, Pennsylvania farmers really suffer.

The Keenes say,

> May the day come soon when people everywhere recognize that a first and significant task is making the land available for those who would use it wisely, and the ordering of our world so that millions of families can once more make a satisfying living from the soil.

The Keenes are in the forefront, demonstrating what Borsodi learned: that "big is bad," "small is human," and "the earth abides."

12
thirty years
at Lane's end homestead

hen one absorbs that a sense of worth, dignity, and responsibility is the key to the quality-life over quantity-life in a new age, one recognizes why the Borsodi pattern of modern homesteading appeals to many thoughtful families. No one knows how many have taken this way in the past twenty (or more) years. No one knows how many have talked with, or read Borsodi, or visited his Dogwoods home or the School of Living, and then fashioned their own family productive home. No one knows many chose this pattern without ever having heard of Borsodi. But each such adventure is a story in itself; each warrants a place in a decentralist revolution.

Here we have space to highlight the life and development of only a few. I include three that grew directly from Ralph Borsodi or his School of Living: 1) the Loomis Lane's End Homestead near Brookville, Ohio, where John and I lived from 1940 through 1970; 2) the Bill and Martha Treichler family who maintained a three-generational homestead from their beginning in 1950 at Birch Lake Farm in Iowa to their present New York homestead, now involving fourth-generational little ones; 3) the 35-year-long versatile and "educational" Sonnewald Homestead of Harold and Grace Lefever, near York, Pennsylvania.

When I left the School of Living in the spring of 1940, I returned to Ohio, and as we had planned, John Loomis and I were married. Our Lane's End thirty acres, five miles south of Brookville, a half-mile off the main road, was the setting for a good life—for John Loomis, his sons and for me—for nearly thirty years.

Seeking improved education for his small motherless sons, (and hampered by conditions on his Missouri farm in 1930) John Loomis had come to Dayton, Ohio. There he and I met on the Liberty Homestead. Following the dissolution of that project in 1935, John bought at auction thirty acres with a run-down cottage (the core being an 1830 log house) and old barn, and a crumbling tobacco shed for $1,050. Here life brought us a new and vital period, largely guided by the School of Living, with which John was in full accord.

Our first adventure the summer of 1940 was refurbishing the cottage. Visiting friends helped us tear out partitions, remove thin ceiling boards with century-old dust falling on us, exposing sturdy hand-hewn beams. Pine-paneling the walls, adding a glistening copper-hooded fireplace, and sanding oak floors completed a rustic enjoyable living center.

Neighbors helped us dig a well; we added plumbing and motors, electrical equipment for grinding flour and cereal, for shredding and juicing and kneading bread; an oven for baking, and in the basement, a washing machine and furnace. We planted a half-acre garden, pruned old fruit trees, repaired the chicken house, shops and barn. In due time, we took down the tobacco shed.

John's pride and joy were his farm animals—his team of Belgians for plowing and haying; his beautiful Jersey cow; several pigs each season, and his small flock of sheep and a flock of chickens. With simple equipment, we farmed the four seven-acre fields and garden. We raised all our grain, all the feed for our animals, our milk and cheese, eggs and meat, vegetables, peaches, apples, pears and berries.

We produced first for our own use, and many a year that totaled 95% of all the food we ate. Sale of a small surplus of soy beans, hay, or corn netted about $1,000 cash each year, which covered gasoline for an old Ford car, electricity, taxes and repairs—and sometimes equipment bought at local farm sales.

Modern homesteading was our delight, and the puzzle of our neighbors. Friends and visitors came frequently; local people couldn't understand so much traffic on our lane. "What do people see in farming that just makes ends meet?" they wondered. They did understand our neighboring farm that took prizes every year at the county fair for the highest yields of corn.

Our "Old Order" neighbor, Howard Brunk, harvested our 7 acres of grain on shares. One day, I met him at the barn gate to take a pan of wheat from the bin of his big machine. I hurried to the kitchen, switched on the electric oven and the small electric mill. Quickly I ground the grain, and mixed the eggs, buttermilk, and several cups of the new flour to make a batter to spoon into muffin tins. I popped it in the hot oven, and soon the good odor told me the muffins were browning. I turned them onto a board, buttered several, and went back to meet Howard, approaching on his second round.

"Want to taste this year's crop?" I asked, handing him a little package.

"All ready to eat? It hasn't been half an hour!...Umm. Good!" he said, biting into one and offering me another. "Best I ever ate," he grinned. "And this wheat hasn't been to Minneapolis or Kansas City—or even through the local mill at Prymont."

We talked some about milling grain at home. When he started his tractor, he called with a cheery salute, "Thanks a lot—and congratulations on the homestead way!"

Several Dayton friends asked if their children might spend a week or a month at Lane's End. To accommodate them, we turned the old milk-house into sleeping and craft quarters. We put in a big window overlooking the creek, and built bunks and benches for as many as six children to extend "our family." They helped in the garden, cared for animals, picked berries, hiked in the woods, and particularly enjoyed natural food at our porch meals. Later, when they were teenagers, they'd come back to reminisce about digging potatoes or harnessing Fanny and driving the small wagon around the pasture.

Friends came too, to discuss our way of life. They arranged to gather informally once a month, as a local School of Living, to examine modern homesteading and decentralism as an alternate "way out" of a cultural decline; they often helped mail our monthly newsletter, the *Interpreter*.

People from a distance stopped by or spent vacations at Lane's End. Many a morning we'd find an out-of-state truck or camper in our barnyard, with someone sleeping to await the dawn. One August day in 1950, we couldn't believe our eyes! A real prairie schooner, a covered wagon was there, with two tethered mules nearby, cropping the grass. June and Farrar Burn, two enthusiastic *Interpreter* readers, had arrived from Bellingham, Washington.

We invited the neighbors over. Farrar regaled us with songs and stories. June told us about her years radioing good nutrition in New York City, and their homesteading on Waldron Island in Puget Sound. They bought their mules and rig to tour the country to see what was happening to people and soils.

They had just discovered Dr. William E. Albrecht in the University of Missouri Agricultural School. "He isn't yet, but surely will be soon, recognized as one of America's greats," June said. "His experiments prove the dependence of human health on the health of the soil, plants, and animals." We welcomed and read the books she showed us: Albrecht's *Soil Fertility and Deficiency Disease*; *Soil Fertility and Sound Teeth*; *Soil Fertility and Democracy*.

"At age 50, I'm going back to college to get an M.A.—in Soil and Nutrition under Dr. Albrecht," June announced.

A treasured book in our library is *Living High*, June's report of the Burns' glorious partnership with nature, in vagabondage from the machine age and money values. With their lives in their own hands, and with a thin pocketbook, the Burns were uncommonly resourceful and lighthearted.

Debt-Free Celebration

Each spring at Lane's End was a joyous season, but in 1946, we had added reason for festivity. We had paid off the mortgage undertaken to buy Lane's End and to remodel our buildings. We planned a dedication with friends on June 30, 1946. We sang "I Am A Tiller Of The Soil, A Farmer Frank And Free." We ate heartily of home-baked bread and fresh salad, and threw off our shoes and danced Seven-Steps on the grass. One guest said, "There's more festivity here and reason for it than any Christmas I can remember."

Each Spring brought its visitors. In 1949 came Ed Robinson and Lyman Wood from Vermont. Like Borsodi, Robinson had a yen for the country, even as a New York advertising man. He was intrigued with the Suffern, New York, School of Living advertising piece, "Have-More Vegetables" and others in the *How To Economize* series. Why not develop a program and really sell these ideas to the public?

With his advertising know-how, Robinson prepared pamphlets on several aspects of homesteading, calling them "The Have-More Plan." During that pleasant visit at Lane's End, they photographed our activities and gathered data. The story of Lane's End in an early issue of their "Have-More Plan" brought more visitors and correspondents.

Lane's End School of Living Building
In the spring of 1950, young Al and Maudie Ebling lived with us. From an Eastern city, they hoped to someday build their homestead "out west." Al heard me talk about a School of Living building for guests and apprentices. "Let's start it," he said. "I'll help, and learn a lot, and you'll have more space for your work."

Fine! A paid-up insurance policy netted us $2,000 cash. We planned a 30'x30' room on the ground floor for meetings, with an adjoining two-story 13'x30' section. We built of concrete, hauling sand and gravel in Al's truck from a nearby quarry. We used an electric mixer and poured concrete into a movable, double-wall aluminum form. We had our problems with floods of rain that prevented pouring; days of no electricity when lines were being repaired; a broken concrete mixer; boils on Al's hands when we women worked alone; broken ropes that dislodged beams we were guiding up inclines! But satisfactions, too: the celebration when our first round of concrete stood five inches high; a 6'x7' pane of glass discovered in a junk yard for our picture window; and friends who came to help. Chief of these was Larry Labadie from Detroit, and Chet Dawson, who had read our newsletter as a GI in the Far North. It was November when these two poured concrete on the top-most round of the second story. To the toast we raised to them that night, Chet rubbed his hands and ruefully responded, "I'm glad I came from Alaska to freeze my fingers for Lane's End School of Living!"

By spring, most of our new building was functioning. In a much-appreciated visit, Ken Kern from Oakhurst, California, installed book shelves and counters for mailing the *Interpreter*.

We decided to memorialize all the love, work, and meaning in this adventure—we would dedicate this building, too. Again, friends came. Ralph Borsodi was there. Speeches were made, our struggles and mistakes laughed about, wise and serious thoughts expressed. But I was too over-whelmed to hear. What had been open space in our cornfield was now en-closed with four walls and a roof! I climbed a ladder to the highest peak of the roof and nailed a leafy twig to represent the Tree of Life gracing our School of Living.

In the fall of 1950, our young niece, Betty, her husband Chuck, and two small children came from the Ozarks to live in our new building. For four years we worked together. Their youngsters grew. Two babies were born, delivered simply and naturally in the pretty, airy bedroom that not long before had been wet concrete. Our friend and Brookville's local physi-cian, Dr. Charles Thomas, attended. A natural birth at home was news in our area. Friends, and friends of friends, heard about it, asking if they could "escape" hospitals and do likewise. In the next five years, seven ba-bies were born naturally in our School of Living building with Dr. Thomas attending.

Having worked with Ralph Borsodi for so long, Lane's Enders were health-conscious. To us, the natural foods from our gardens, fields, or-chard and dairy, plus the exercise in producing them, were constant sources of well-being. Our discussion of them in our monthly journal brought interesting response.

When our friend Myrtle-Mae Borsodi discovered she had a cancerous breast, we were greatly concerned. I accompanied her to Dr. Max Gerson, a German physician in America offering a whole-food, high-potassium, low-sodium diet to heal and avoid surgery. He arranged for an hourly program of fresh carrot and apple juice, alternating with celery-cabbage and green drink; baked potatoes, steamed greens, cottage cheese, no meat, and dilute potassium liquid. I followed it too—and found it refreshing and invigorating.

Friends shared their experience with similar treatments. In an effort to research and understand them, I experimented with them. Over the years, I have enjoyed working with various persons and their ideas, including Dr. Ann Wigmore's wheat grass; Dr. Ernest Shearer's plumb-bob test; Herbert Armstrong's remarkable organic farm at Sandy Point, Texas; Dr. Mason Rose's hair analysis; Dr. Harry Alsleben's chelation; Dr. Bernard Jensen's iridology; reflexology; yoga; acupuncture; and so on.

Conferences and Official Incorporation

At Lane's End, we organized annual regional and national decentralist conferences: at Bloomington, Illinois, in 1949; at Troy Mills, Iowa, in 1950; at Earlham College, Richmond, Indiana, in 1951 and 1952; at Wittenberg College, Springfield, Ohio, in 1953; in St. Louis in 1954. To them we invited persons in various New Age, alternative culture groups to lecture and lead discussions, to exhibit their wares and books. Responding were Dr. Joe Nichols of Natural Food Associates, Noah Alper of the Georgists, Griscom Morgan of Community Service, Dr. Edwin Wilson of the Humanist Association, Daisy Wingfield of the Gesell money reform, Dr. Jonathan Forman of Friends of the Land and Organic Farming; teachers of natural childbirth, breast feeding, Montessori, Steiner and Summerhill education, and many others. The cross-fertilization of ideas was reported by Robert West Howard of the Pathfinder and Christian Science Monitor, by F.H. Behymer of the St. Louis Dispatch, and other national journals in the 1950s.

In 1954, members of our Ohio informal School of Living voted to become an official nation-wide School of Living for adult education. We applied, and were incorporated as an educational non-profit group in Ohio on July 5, 1954. The charter and by-laws repeated the purpose and structure of the Borsodi School of Living at Suffern, New York, an association of artists, craftsmen, and teachers to study and teach how to live like normal (fully-functioning) human beings.

DECENTRALISM

Our educational work was part of our life at Lane's End. Our School of Living building was headquarters for editing and mailing the *Green Revolution* and for organizing the nationwide decentralist conferences for the decade 1946–1956.

Visitors and apprentices joined in our activities. Among the long-term apprentices in the 50s and 60s were Ray and Lila Russ from Florida (whose search I reported in *Go Ahead And Live*); Don Werkheiser from Connecticut, Bruce and Betty Elwell from Philadelphia, Ferdi and Becky Knoess from Chicago, Bob and Arlen Wilson of New York City. All worked for and helped edit our journals, *Balanced Living* and *Green Revolution*.

Letters flowed in and out, asking and answering questions. Particularly treasured were beautiful hand-scripted approving ones from Lewis Mumford. Authors sent books and pamphlets, and our postmaster suggested we install a larger mail box at the end of the lane.

Lane's End Homestead and its School of Living, until John's death in 1968, was our bond with hundreds of Green Revolutionaries.

13
treichler's three generation homesteads

Bill Treichler, a young veteran of World War II, was challenged by Ralph Borsodi's decentralism. On his family farm in Troy Mills, Iowa, Bill's efforts to incorporate Borsodi's concept of a three-generation family, adapted to a Midwest farm situation, makes history in the decentralist revolution.

Bill Treichler had met Borsodi in the 1946 decentralist conference in Bloomington, Illinois. A few years later, courting his bride-to-be, Martha, at Black Mountain College, he suggested she read Borsodi's *Education and Living*.

In the fall of 1948, Bill and Martha arranged for Borsodi to visit their campus. Most of the students had never heard of Borsodi, and they questioned and disagreed with him. But disarmed by his quiet good nature, even hostile students were won by the force of his ideas; many became admirers. Martha was as enthusiastic as Bill—they decided to marry and develop their own homestead with Bill's parents on Birch Lake Farm

In 1950, they married and moved in. Bill contributed farm equipment he had bought with his Air Force savings. Their first step was to design and build a home for themselves. Like Borsodi's, their home should have an area for home production—a compact, efficient kitchen with plenty of work-space for food preparation and preservation. Bill's father suggested they make a model, so they could view their home from every angle.

DECENTRALISM

Led and reinforced by what they read in Borsodi's books and the School of Living's monthly *Interpreter*, the brick and glass home, with a pole roof, came into being across the lawn from the main house at the edge of Birch Lake. Martha and Bill skinned poles, dug ditches, cleaned old brick and laid them up. The senior Treichlers helped too. Sometimes they sat around the table talking things over, especially when they didn't agree on the next steps. The new house was ready to move into at the end of the year, and by then, baby Rachel moved in with them. For the first time, the Treichler homestead was three-generational.

Bill and Martha were enthusiastic about organic farming, decentralism, and proper nutrition, gleaned from the *Interpreter*, *Organic Gardening*, and Lady Eve Balfour's *The Living Soil*. Meeting writers of these at decentralist conferences greatly stimulated their ideas. The elder Treichlers were tolerant—but not enthusiastic.

In return for Bill and Martha's garden produce, the older Treichlers helped with clothing for the growing children. Grandmother Treichler turned out stylish dresses, shirts, overalls, winter coats and mittens from adult worn-out garments. She taught Martha to sew, and Rachel too had her sewing lessons from her grandmother.

Bill and Martha's children helped with homestead jobs when they were five and six years old. By ten, they sold strawberries and sweet corn of their own. In the winter they carried wood for fireplace, cookstove, and furnace. They joined the 4-H Club, and from their own garden, exhibited products at the county fair. They earned real tools of their own. By teen-age, they bought more to add to their individual collections. But acquisitions didn't accrue fast—one summer, all together, they earned just enough to buy themselves a second-hand freezer.

Grandfather's standards for children were high. The children enjoyed watching him work, and he encouraged their interest. When the children littered the lawn with old oil drums and boards for shacks, with tricycles and wagons and recent finds from the farm junk pile, the grandparents were often disturbed. The solution—give the children their own space, sheltered from view by a barn and by trees, where they could build to their hearts' content.

Some serious disagreements came from differences in attitudes about farming as a business. The parents, particularly Mother Treichler, thought the young Treichlers should earn money by farming for products to sell. Bill thought they could earn more by producing their own living on the farm. Martha joined him in wanting to concentrate on being as independent as possible of money.

In the early years of their marriage, they spent only about $5.00 a month on food. The farm supplied all the wheat, corn, milk, butter, cheese, eggs, beef, fruits and vegetables. Some years, they raised cane for sorghum. The woods supplied firewood and logs to put through their saw mill for building. From their fields, they sold soybeans, hogs and cattle, and later, whole-wheat flour, corn meal, and frozen beef and pork. In general, they followed two methods—raising as much as they could for their own use and also selling products for cash.

In the 1950s, Bill and Martha kept close contact with friends in the School of Living for support and inspiration for their way of life. To some of their neighbors and nearby friends, self-sufficient homesteading was a retrogression, a return to "horse-and-buggy days." But Bill and Martha shared Borsodi's vision that it was much more—that their homestead was a creative way of living with the advantages of an extended family, and an efficient and human part of a decentralized economy. For them, the School of Living way was an enjoyable, worthwhile adventure.

In 1954, the Treichlers joined in sponsoring the School of Living conference in their home town, Troy Mills, Iowa, population 950. Nearly all the people in the community had a part in it, listening to Ralph Borsodi interpret the philosophy supporting rural, self-sufficient three-generational living in the modern day. I described Lane's End Homestead in Ohio; Ralph and Rose Smart brought a film on clothing design; Tim Lefever described his low-cost building with solar heat at Sonnewald Homestead.

Two more children were born at Birch Lake Homestead. They grew on its food, played in its woods, explored its fields and lake. They became close friends with people in the community, and with distant ones who came to visit. Martha was a 4-H leader for five years; they took time to read, study, and make things for their house.

DECENTRALISM

As the children grew, they doubled the size of their cottage and still they needed more room. If they invested further in the house, could they buy the farm? But their parents were not ready to sell. United States Army Corps of Engineers was proposing a dam downstream on the Wapsipicon that might completely flood their farm. Bill, Martha and family decided reluctantly to make a change.

Bill applied to be farm manager at the Colorado Rocky Mountain School, and was accepted. The family would stay together in the country, the children attending the mountain school. They spent two happy years there before the school phased out its organic farming.

The Treichlers then moved to a similar school at Vershire, Vermont, to teach as well as to look after the school farm and garden. Four of their five children have graduated from Vershire Mountain School; three have gone on to college. Martha has earned an M.A. degree from a nearby college.

When Bill's parents died, Bill and Martha received a cash inheritance. With that, plus savings, Bill's family bought 88 acres on a hilltop in New York's rural lake country. They went homesteading the second time.

They have been happy on the new homestead. Each of the youngsters has projects they had not been able to have until the family again had land of their own. The children have been equipped and trained for this adventure—philosophically, emotionally, materially. The daughters make nearly all their own clothes, including coats. Joe, the oldest boy, also makes some of his own, including a carefully-tailored leather jacket and trousers.

Rachel owns all her own tools and office equipment for creative silver-smithing and free-lance photography. Two sons, still in college, own hand tools collected at auctions, as well as a new metal lathe and a used crawler-tractor with a backhoe. Seventeen-year-old Barbara works her large antique loom and spinning wheel, a treasured graduation present.

The Treichler family are committed to their second three-generation homestead. On it, the children are assured of help and hospitality. Both parents and children agree on the importance—even necessity—of each person having individual choice and sovereignty within a three-generation family.

They look forward to each child using a part of the family homestead to continue the three-generation pattern. They say:

> We agree with Borsodi that one's first need is to assume responsibility for our own survival—to avoid being parasitic. To accept and fulfill our gift of life is integrity.
>
> To be both productive and sovereign calls for land and life in the country. To create something better than ourselves, we need to nourish and foster growth in our children. This is parenthood, our link with the past and the future.
>
> Homesteading integrates both inner forces and external aspects. We have discovered that surviving and living in this way inevitably makes a person compassionate and a creator and admirer of beauty. We recommend three-generational homesteading for a good life.

14

sonnewald:
self sufficiency, home-industry
and social outreach

he Lefever Family's Sonnewald Homestead near Spring Grove, Pennsylvania, demonstrates other aspects of modern decentralist life ways. They not only produce 70 to 80% of their food, but instead of selling surplus agricultural products, they earn their cash by two services operated on their homestead. One is Harold's (Tim's) electrical and plumbing repair service; the other is Grace's nutrition and natural food store. Both qualify for the term "cottage industry," now becoming common in decentralist circles.

Sonnewald Homestead merits its name, Sunny Woods. Sixty acres of grassy fields and strips of woods encircle a small pond. At the center, is a cluster of several modern buildings where this busy family lives and works. Sonnewald provides for the Lefever family itself, and often for many more guests and apprentices. It is also the setting from which their activities contribute to the wider good society.

The Lefever's first goal, and their achievement as well, is a high level of self-sufficiency. Someone works every day of the year mulching, tilling, planting, pruning, feeding, or harvesting in their several acres of orchards, berries, and gardens. Rows of lettuce and endive are planted in early spring and autumn to become summer and winter salads and "green drinks." Sheltered greens and root crops are uncovered and used fresh from under winter snow, or from root cellars. At harvest time, freezers and refrigerators are full with summer fruit and vegetables. Celery, cabbage, mounds of carrots, beets, turnips. potatoes cover the root-cellar floor. Someone is always busy in the kitchen preparing, processing, or consuming their own good natural food.

There's nothing isolated, withdrawn, or back-woods about Sonnewald Homestead. Almost any day there's a surprising interaction of people, concerns, organizations, movements. From the mail box there's a daily armload of magazines, books, letters; scores of telephone calls are handled, with conversation and transactions completed while Grace, phone resting on her shoulder, chops salad or puts carrots through the juicer.

Committees meet there several times a month, planning for local, state, and national activities. Visitors arrive daily for consultation on nutrition, solar and wind energy, ecology, organic gardening, composting, civil rights, economic reform, and so on. Customers arrive, too, for Tim's plumbing business, or to shop in Grace's health-food and book shop.

A day I spent at Sonnewald is typical. Actually, my day began the night before. Along with many others, I arrived early at the monthly meeting of the York Natural Food and Health Association, of which Tim and Grace were principal officers. Tonight's subject: A World Without Cancer.

Unloading from their station wagon, the five Lefevers carried in boxes and books. Dan and Nancy setup the literature table while Grace and Tim got the meeting underway for a standing-room audience.

The program featured an hour-length film on *A World Without Cancer*, showing the difference between well-nourished and poorly-nourished human cells. In the latter, toxins and poisons are not eliminated. Decades of excess body-toxins irritate normal cells, and the body responds with an over-balance of estrogen, which further disturbs metabolism and causes uninhibited growth of cells called cancer. The conclusion? That cancer is deficiency, a degeneration, a disease of civilization, in which packaged, processed and devitalized food has a prominent part.

In addition, the film showed the effect from the use of Vitamin B17 or amygdaline, made from apricot pits. In the body, this extract releases hydrogen-cyanide, which inhibits, arrests, and destroys cancer cells. We saw the vigorous Hunzas in the Himalayas, among whom a case of cancer has never been found—a major item of their diet is apricots.

DECENTRALISM

In the film, dozens of cancer patients were interviewed before and after their use of B17 extract. At the end of the meeting en route to the Lefever homestead, Tim said, "Couldn't get people to start home—it's the latest we've ever been."

"And one of the largest crowds," Dan said. "Nearly a third of them newcomers and first-timers."

"A lot of them took free literature, or bought a book," Nancy added.

"And York's leading physician was there," Grace exulted. "He didn't say anything, but he bought a book on "A World Without Cancer."

We tumbled into bed after midnight, and woke with the phone ringing. "Wonderful meeting! Congratulations!" a neighbor greeted Grace. Several times an hour someone called adding their enthusiasm, or asking, "Why haven't we known this before?"

Nancy missed her school bus, and Grace chauffeured her to the village. Harold went off on a schedule of repairs. Grace returned to greet customers at the store. Mark, an apprentice, ground fresh flour, cut beautiful cheese, packed nuts and fruit. Dan plowed out the summer's onions. I picked lima beans and pears for drying. The steady low heat in the drying oven was just right to take the chill from the house until the sun warmed the solar panels on the second floor.

While Grace set out good bread, cheese and apple-sauce for lunch and prepared her weekly order for health foods, Tim and I talked of his past, present, and future goals. "Did you grow up on a farm?" I asked him.

"No—our forebears were farmers, but my family lived in York. My roots go back to the French Huguenots to war and tyranny; they left us a legacy of resistance to much that produces war in the modern system. Our geneology shows Sonnewald Lefevers as the eleventh generation descendants of Mengen Lefever, who settled with others in the central Pennsylvania hills."

"What influenced you most as a young person?"

"My father was a mechanic, and I learned his skills, followed his interests, and read all the science and mechanic journals I could find. I was headed for an electrician's apprenticeship. I had no trouble making good grades in school."

"You mean you were first in everything," interrupted Grace, "and finished electrical engineering at Penn State in three and a half years."

"Was that where you got your plan for solar heating your home?"

"No, that came later. But I did get a technical and engineering background. War had been declared when I was ready for a job. Several contracts were available. But all involved war work, and were not compatible with my pacifism. Westinghouse seemed the least objectionable, and I took a job with them in Pittsburgh."

"What did you do when the U.S. entered the war, and you had to register for the draft?"

"I registered, but declared my objection to war. They allowed me a conscientious objector's position. But when I was called later, I refused to report to conscientious objector camp. This, of course, was illegal, and I faced prison. In June, 1942, Jane and I were married; the next day, officers came and took me off for arraignment, and later to prison for draft refusal. But Jane was a plucky bride, stood it well, and did her part in anti-war education."

"Did your prison years have an impact?" I asked.

"Yes, very special. I made friends with several outstanding conscientious objectors, and came upon a monthly paper, *Brethren Action*, which you, Mildred, and a few Ohio Church of The Brethren people were writing. It was an analysis of war and pacifism, and in advance of the official denomination's position. You were espousing rural life, decentralism, and interpreting Ralph Borsodi's work."

"I studied every copy," he went on. "Still have them filed away. I don't believe anything equals the effect that Borsodi's ideas had on me. They put together what I saw, felt, and believed. From them, I began to be motivated toward self-sufficient and homestead living. Several other fellows in prison also saw the homestead life as consistent with non-violence and pacifism."

"How and when did you develop Sonnewald Homestead?"

"I bought our 60 acres in 1944, and put up a Quonset hut with one all-glass side, facing south—a crude beginning of solar heating. Jane and I lived in it seven years, and our first three children were born there. We lost

Jane when the children were little. Grace and I were married a few years later, and we moved into our present solar-heated home."

"Will you explain your solar-heating system? Did you design it?"

"I found a plan in *Popular Science*—one of the earliest discussions of solar heat—designed by Maria Telkes of Massachusetts Institute of Technology. I showed her my adaptations of it, and she approved my using her fundamental design. Basically, it calls for a second story with high, double or thermo-paned windows, facing south, with proper roof overhang that permits maximum use of winter sun, and minimum summer sun. Back of the exposed panels is a thin steel sheet painted black. Enclosing the six-inch chamber behind the steel sheeting is an insulated board wall. The steel sheet is heated when the sun shines, as is the air in the narrow chamber on each side of the steel. Maximum temperature is about 140 degrees. A thermostat on the ground floor regulates the fans which blow warmed air to the first floor. We have had supplementary heat from a heatolator fireplace, now a Franklin stove, and also from a small oil-heater. We heat the core of our 65'x30' house at low cost, entirely satisfactory to our needs."

"How do you rate the cost and energy used for fuel?"

"Actually, our fuel bills run only about $100 a year. The ecology department at Dickinson College in Carlisle did a survey of energy used in four homes of comparable size. Our home used the lowest amount of all, while a modern suburban home used almost double, as did a cooperative student house. I figure that over the years, our family has used as little energy from irreplaceable sources as almost anyone else in the country. It's a good feeling to be part of lightening the burden."

"Any other features of Sonnewald you'd rank as important as your solar heating?"

"I think our compost heap belongs there. That big area of leaves breaking down may not be the most scientifically-layered compost, but it is always ready for mulching our trees, berries, and gardens, as well as being tilled into the soil. They're hauled here each year by the York Street Department, and we're glad to pay the small cost for each firmly-pressed load of many tons."

"What influenced you to do all that?"

"Long ago, we were inspired by the way the Chinese had kept soil fertile for 4,000 years. They used every bit of vegetable waste. All that leaf mold has helped Sonnewald in that direction for over thirty years. Our soil grows increasingly organic.

"And with all this, you've also been active with the School of Living," I exclaimed.

"Having been influenced by Borsodi and you, Mildred, at Lane's End in the beginning, we followed that pattern. We're listed as one of the 'centers' of the School of Living. We've been members and often officers of the School since the early 1940s. I've been president of the Board of Trustees several times, and Grace has been chairman too. The whole family attends the School's conferences, and we helped move the School's headquarters from Ohio here to the East in the 1960s."

"Are your summer conferences part of the School of Living program?"

"Yes, several times each summer, a group of forty people studies and shares our activities for a three-day weekend. People appreciate it, and along with volley-ball, swimming, and folk games, we all have a good time. We must have had 500 people over the last five years—we continually hear of the homesteads those people have developed all over the states, and the community action they're doing."

"What about those mobile homes on the slope beyond the orchard?"

"They might suggest a trailer court, but actually, they help Sonnewald express a very old and basic principle of the School of Living good-life concept—that of the expanded and three-generation family. Those trailers have made it possible for my parents and older aunts and uncles to live here with us. They helped care for the babies and youngsters, and our children have been glad to have Grandpa and Grandma close by. They and the children would shell peas, string beans, make Christmas decorations, go on bird walks. And we helped care for them when they were sick, we shared their lives, and mourned their deaths when they left us."

"A far cry from an old people's home!" I remarked.

"Yes—I agree with Borsodi when he says the family probably came into existence to care for the elderly as much as to care for children."

"And your adolescents—how does Sonnewald appeal to them?"

DECENTRALISM

"We and they look upon youth as a time for venturing out of the home nest, but returning to it at any time of need. Our children have followed this pattern. The boys have married quite early—Bart and his bride lived with us for a while, and Evan and Sharon are back now, helping me with windmill research, and building a new storage barn. Willa is traveling, and right now is in an Iowa commune. We'll all enjoy having her back home when she arrives."

Tim excused himself. "A job needs doing before I leave for a meeting of the Pennsylvania Organic Farmer/Consumer Organization in Harrisburg."

Nancy came in from school, fixed herself a sprout-and-tomato sandwich, and began preparing the main-dish for supper—a mammoth bowl of cut greens, beets, carrots, and cucumbers.

"Have you a plan for yourself when you are out of school?" I asked.

"Yes, I want to be a teacher."

"So, you have some teacher whom you admire and want to be like?"

"Yes, my Mom," she replied.

In a day noted for its generation gap, Nancy's reply testifies to the success of the Sonnewald Homestead. Many visitors, apprentices, and third-generation residents value their experience there. They are aware of lacks, problems, and imbalances. Some find it strenuous, others find it hectic. But the benefits are clear.

When others are threatened by shortages, the Lefevers have more than enough. When energy is being wasted, they are heated by the sun and powered by the wind. When people are weak and sick, they have no need for doctors and nurses. When others are lonely and deprived, they enjoy family, neighbors, friends. When others are apathetic or helpless, they are interacting almost daily with important groups for social change in civil rights, War Resisters, natural foods, the Church of the Brethren, Georgists, ecologists, the School of Living and its Land Trusts. When millions trek to monotonous jobs in factories and offices, the Lefevers work creatively at their own pace on their own homestead.

15
Decentralist technics:
peter vanDresser

n the early School of Living days, 1936–1940, Peter vanDresser was a frequent and welcome participant. A creative architect and engineer by profession, he was giving thought to strategic and emerging decentralist technology. His cogent analyses and recommendations often appeared in the decentralist journal *Free America*. So clearly did vanDresser predict the energy crisis (of the 1970s) and outline alternatives that his comments were republished verbatim years later (1975), by *Mother Earth News*. (I quote and summarize from that article, and later include his comments on "The Incomplete Decentralist.")

For a decade, Peter vanDresser lived on a homestead in Florida, and in 1949, moved to the New Mexican Rockies to "integrate with a deeply-rooted local community, and to grow with that community, rather than start a brand-new intentional society, or to demonstrate a largely illusory self-sufficiency." Through the years, he continued writing and giving counsel. Several times he joined Buckminster Fuller in programs. In 1977, he spent four months in Europe talking with groups of decentralist persuasion.

In 1938, in "Technics of Decentralization," he said we were in a Power Age, rather than in an Industrial Age. He emphasized the centralizing effect of stationary coal/steam power. He pointed to the decrease and approaching exhaustion of petroleum reserves. Since the manufacture of automobiles—the greatest Power Age industry and keystone of our economic

DECENTRALISM

structure—is dependent on this supply, drastic reorganization in both our technology and economy is to be expected. Almost 95% of the mechanical power in this country is used in transportation, and most of that in trucks and automobiles. The Power Age is also a Transportation Age.

The answers predicted in 1938 by Peter vanDresser for the petroleum shortage included extracting oil from shale, an increasing use of coal, the harnessing of all available water power, and the production of alcohol from crops as an alternative fuel, along with power from the wind, tides, the sun, and geothermal sources. Even these would not be altogether adequate, he said. Synthesized oil or alcohol would be more costly than oil from gushers; coal would be harder to come by; all the falling waters in the country would meet only a fraction of the current energy needs; wind power is not adaptable to many industrial uses.

Peter vanDresser predicted that to power consumption would be added the question, "Is power doing work which needs to be done at all? Could it be eliminated under an economic arrangement more logical than finance capitalism? Why should railroads proudly reveal that the average potato travels 741 miles from the field to the corner grocery? For railroads, this may be a good thing—but a very bad thing for an efficient use of coal and mineral resources.

Like Ralph Borsodi, vanDresser emphasized local 'production and use' of many goods, and the decentralization of social practices. Much of the horsepower used in transportation would be unnecessary in a decentralized and well-rounded regional development. The ultimately practical solution of the power problem lies in decentralizing America.

Hydro-electricity is almost the lifeblood of the modern trend toward decentralization and a life-technic economy. It breaks down the old coal-and-steam concentrations of factories and population. Electricity distributes power over wire through the countryside, facilitating conservation; a mine often blights a countryside. Small dams, properly engineered and constructed, can control floods, drought, erosion.

Wind-driven electric plants are best adapted to light-industrial or domestic use, and are an important part of a distributist/decentralist technology.

106

In many ways, alcohol is superior to gasoline—burns more cleanly, is adapted to high compression, with less heat loss. When the rising cost of petroleum puts the cost of gasoline 1/3 more than alcohol distilled from starch crops, it will make alcohol feasible. Since it is dependent on farming, not mining, for its crude material, alcohol production would push the economy toward an agrarian (though not necessarily decentralized) operation. Solar heat will be used to run steam engines, operate refrigerating units, and to generate gas for cooking. Its most practical use is in heating domestic water.

Arthur Pound said in 1936, "The most important business of mankind has been putting power, more power, and ever more power, behind wheels for increasing convenience and prosperity of society." Peter vanDresser calls this attitude the *infancy* rather than the wisdom, of science.

Short of the use of atomic energy (which would be an absolute major catastrophe), vanDresser said, "We shall be forced by natural laws to revise our attitude toward machines, energy, and power. We shall be forced to develop a kind of technic closely related to the natural cycles of land, water, air, and living matter—applied more judiciously and efficiently than is done today." But there is no lack of supply. America's farming lands can supply not less than 7% billions of horsepower. More and more technics must refine this titanic laboratory, and fewer and fewer concern themselves with an attack on the bowels of the earth and ever-more-powerful contrivances.

Still as we enter the uncertain 80s, Peter vanDresser supports the relative independence of families on modern homesteads, but deplores the concept that evolved to almost a "cult of primitive self-sufficiency." Among the 1960 "communiteers," many young people held notions of flight to the wilderness, and a return to a new tribalism and to the womb of "mother earth."

In their New Mexico center near Santa Fe, the vanDressers encountered increasing numbers of drop-outs from psychedelic enclaves in San Francisco, New York, and their various megalopolitan suburbs, who were trying to live out these fantasies. While sympathetic with their unhappiness with the financial/industrial "establishment," and their desires for an alternative lifestyle, vanDresser could not disregard the fumbling, fragmented, and often self-defeating qualities of their efforts to achieve such an alternative.

Particularly in contrasting these efforts with the patient continuity of the Old Mexico villages in the region, vanDresser became aware of the inadequacy of the one-track do-it-yourself 'each in his own bag' approaches of many of the new "pioneers." VanDresser noted that "this cast of mind seemed to predominate even the communes where people appeared banded together more in mutual hostility to the square world, with a grudging minimum of cooperation amongst themselves for bare survival, rather than a generous sense of mutual humanity."

This sort of *reductio ad absurdum* of the earlier concepts of American independence and self-reliance seemed to vanDresser to be hindering rather than aiding evolution toward a more-balanced ecologically-viable society. Even a simple economy requires a degree of specialization and organization in order to achieve necessary technology. The hardiest pioneer cannot mine, refine, and forge the iron for his axe. Fragmented individuals cannot achieve this degree of social structure.

Soon after settling in a several-hundred-years-old village of Spanish-speaking people in the Southwest, vanDresser realized that,

> The strategic kind of pioneering needed at this time was in terms of community, not of individual survival and self-reliance. Even a degree of community self-reliance, at most partial and relative, must be balanced with a wholesome exchange and relationship with the locality, the region, and the world.

For such reasons, vanDresser began to think that the restorative process needed in our society could be better called "recentralization" rather than "decentralization," but recentralization on a scale compatible with real human needs and with the facts of energy and conservation of natural resources.

Peter and Florence vanDresser, as immigrants into a new land, decided to integrate with a deeply-rooted local community, to grow and evolve with that community, rather than to start a new project. This has proven to be a "long, slow, and unspectacular process, with its successes modest, diffused, and often ambiguous, with many and repeated frustrations."

A large part of their effort has been the prosaic business of working out a means of livelihood which meshes reasonably well with, and which enriches, the local economy. In their case, this was primarily a small village restaurant, using personally-, locally-, and regionally-produced food. This included some aspects of the classical homesteading pattern, in that they built homes and other buildings after learning the native techniques. They also raised some of their own food, and gathered fuel wood in the nearby National Forest.

They cooperated with villagers constructing the local water system, helped with the irrigation ditches, and participated in a community school. From time to time, "higher level" activities were called for, such as serving on State advisory committees for various development and improvement programs.

In recent years, vanDresser has promoted low technology, or folk-level use of solar energy in the region, as one of the founding members of the New Mexico Solar Energy Association. The small solar house he built in 1958 in Santa Fe is now rated the second-oldest continually functioning solar residence in the country.

He has participated in a number of seminars on rural and solar development, and has written two books: *A Landscape for Humans* and *Homegrown Sundwellings*, published by Lightning Tree Press, Santa Fe. These are constructive contributions to decentralist and biotechnic development in this and other parts of the world. Florence and Peter vanDresser now sense a rootedness and a belonging in a beautiful part of the country which, in this day and age, is not easy to come by.

16

ken keRn:
líttle Davío among gíant Buílders

Ken Kern of Oakhurst, California, another life-member of the School of Living, has for twenty-five years lived and breathed life-oriented technology. He has designed and built several homes for his family; he has designed and helped in the building of hundreds of other homes and homesteads. He does not encounter any piece of land that his imagination does not immediately see on it people and animals, houses and buildings to fit the landscape, gardens and wood lots to build the soil, and all manner of new cost-saving decentralist technology such as indoor greenhouses, original housing units, fireplaces, compost privies, etc.

Next to the food industry, building and construction is the largest of all modern industries. Government, corporate, and contractor-building have flashed to become giant enterprises. Yet many Americans retain their do-it-yourself attitudes, and dream of building their own homes. Of the millions who dream, 160,000 persons achieved their self-built home in 1970.

Through his books, *Owner-Built Home* (1961) and *Owner-Built Homestead (1972)*, Ken Kern has influenced many builders. For thirty years, he has been the little David contending with building Goliaths. His life has a Horatio Alger flavor.

In his student days at the University of Oregon (1947–1950), Ken was guided by Dr. Ernest Guyon to a decentralist owner-built philosophy. He left college imbued with creating his own home and homestead from

110

scratch. Hitch-hiking down the Pacific Coast in 1950, Ken was given a lift by Morgan Harris, then professor of economics at Chapman College. Their exchange of views revealed a common concern in, and understanding of, the importance of decentralization.

"You belong, Ken," Morgan said to him, "in the School of Living, founded by Ralph Borsodi. You should read its journal the *Interpreter*." Thus began a correspondence uninterrupted to this day between Ken Kern and myself.

In 1952, Ken bought for $600 twenty acres of open land in the low Sierras near Oakhurst, California. He built temporary, but artistic, shelter, and began developing the land, designing, and constructing his unconventional housing and homesteading. He married, and his growing family added incentive, help, and satisfaction to his life work.

Ken's first visit to Lane's End Homestead was in 1952, when he added hours of work to the School of Living building. He wrote items — always appreciated by readers of the School's journals. The School of Living published his first reports, which he later compiled and republished as *The Owner-Built Home*. His philosophy, methods, and achievements were constant stimulation.

As the disaffection with industrialism increased in the 50s and 60s, *Mother Earth News* came on the scene. It republished Kern's *The Owner-Built Home* and a bulge developed in his outreach. He set up his own publishing business on his homestead, and there prepared and published "Owner-Builder Publications." To find isolation for his work, the Kerns sought a retreat to a lesser-known spot. Reports indicate annual sales of Owner-Builder books have grown to tens of thousands of dollars; Scribners asked to republish *The Owner-Built Home* in a $13 hard-cover-edition.

In the summer of 1975, Ken's book, in collaboration with Rob Thnallon and Ted Kogon, *The Code: Politics of Building Your Own Home* is a dynamite presentation of what is wrong with, and what can be done about, injustices in building regulations as they affect owner-builders. Of 200 pages, 40 show homes built by owners outside code regulations. In

Mendocino County, California, 600 such homes provide adequate shelter for the families who built them.

Ever inventing and improving, Ken and Barbara Kern in 1977 bought 80 open acres for a new life-centered laboratory in home-building. On it, they plan to construct demonstration homesteads with buildings of wood, stone, concrete, adobe, with gardens and outbuildings, embodying the best features of the various methods they have discovered over the years.

Ken Kern has risen to an innovative, popular builder and successful author. His future seems unlimited. But Ken Kern has always been, and will remain, a good homesteader, a thorough decentralist, and a supporter of the American dream of independent owner-built homes.

The following pages from an article published in a 1975 issue of the School of Living's *Green Revolution* describes the philosophy, method, and status of Owner-Built technology in the U.S.

Revolution In Housing by Ken Kern

Until very recently, Progress in house-building meant a blind faith in the unremitting expansion of the industry. Now we are turning to zero household growth. We are re-ordering our priorities, changing our cultural values, and reducing our demands on natural resources. A new-era economy in construction is on the threshold in North America, coupled with a concern for using natural materials and energy resources.

The traditional symbol of the good life in America has been the detached single-family home. But out of eight house-needy families, only one has been able to pay for its own home. Over 25% in this country depend on governmental financial assistance for housing, either through direct subsidy or property-tax relief.

But free enterprise is building, too. The building industry has put up great numbers of planned, high-density housing developments, yet has failed to include necessary energy-saving and material conserving methods. The industry has promoted modular, mobile, pre-fabricated factory produced housing. All this is not sensitive to emerging lifestyles which reject the machine-made solution to *human need for organic housing.*

Shelter needs continue to grow. Most single family houses are bought by the 25-44 years-old age-group. From 1960 to 1970, this group was 20% of the population of the U.S., by 1980, it will be 30%. Over 3,000,000 new houses are needed in this country in the next ten years, with fewer people who can afford to buy one.

Owner-Built Homes

Human beings are complex creatures with physical, emotional, and intellectual needs and capacities. Living in, and building, their homes should satisfy these needs and develop these capacities. None of these owner-needs is expressed in factory produced housing, and only impersonally in contractor-built units at excessive cost. No one can create a house fulfilling a person's total environmental needs better than the persons who live in that environment. An owner-built home can join site and ecology; can express one's own concept of aesthetics and design; can facilitate one's own particular life-style, and use available, native energy, resources, and materials. Accordingly, I have designed, and explain here, a house that owner-builders can use as a guide, and adapt to personal situations.

The aim is maximum self-sufficient energy, primarily the sun. On south-facing walls, during summer, shading devices exclude unwanted high-angle rays. During winter, they admit the sun's desirable low-angle warming rays. Through the large window areas, heat from winter sun is absorbed by dark slate-covered floors of the living area, where captive heat will be stored for nighttime re-radiation. For winter, too, sun-heated water from the attached sun-pit greenhouse adds

113

supplemental heat. Mechanical air-conditioners and room-coolers are dispensed with. Prevailing breezes are used. The high, large, leeward-opening vents and the low, small, windward-opening vents of exterior walls furnish maximum velocity of interior air-flow.

My model would use a wind generator to produce electrical energy. In North America, they show great promise as simple, efficient, low-cost power sources. The wind-generator will help bring cheaper, outlying marginal lands into use by owner-builders. (Commercial power costs severely limit building and building-sites.) Main fuel source for space-heating, cooking, and water in the owner-built prototype is wood. A few-acre wood lot on the site provides a sustained yield of fuel. An efficient heat-circulating fireplace and a thermostatically-controlled heater-stove provide adequate back-up heat for the entire house. In both fireplace and stove are supplementary water-heating coils. A wood-fired sauna is in the upper-level bathing facility.

A composting system recycles all organic wastes with minimum water, in a sealed chamber directly below the toilet, with outside clean out. Bathing and washing water flows through drain tile to replenish groundwater. In some regions, water should be collected from a single-pitch roof, and stored in an adjacent cistern. The five-gallon toilet flush is reduced to one-quart of water in the compost-privy drop. Water conserving foot-operated mist sprays are used for bathing. Front loading clothes washers use half as much water as top loading ones. Pressure-regulated shower heads (for sauna bathing) reduce water use. Wash-water can be recycled by circulating through a simple, roof-mounted solar still. Having plumbing fixtures concentrated in one area reduces installation and maintenance costs, and saves both hot and cold water.

For insulation, earth is piled high against cold, north facing walls. Since ground temperatures are constant at 45°-60°F.

a few feet below the surface, earth berming offers heating and cooling advantages. An 8-inch covering of earth and sod on the roof equals 4 inches of fiberglass. Slab floors at ground-level use seasonally-stored earth-heat. An under-the-floor "no draft" system distributes fireplace and stove heat throughout the house. Floor heat, in sunny days, is thus circulated to other parts of the house.

Climate and Esthetic Features

People-impact on the eco-system should be minimized. For optimum comfort, the house should be on a south-facing slope of about 10 to 15 degrees. An established windbreak of mixed conifers and deciduous trees should be north of the house, with sufficient natural ground-cover everywhere to prevent erosion. The shape of the house maximizes solar exposure, minimizing heat loss.

The basic shell of the prototype house is lean, clean, and simple enough for an unskilled owner-builder to construct. It requires less skill, fewer tools, less time and energy than most plans. The interior is an "open plan," with few walls and less floor areas. A sleeping loft reduces roof and foundation. Movable screens articulate use-areas. When not used, space can be closed off. Work areas have long, high, horizontally-placed windows for necessary light. At night and in cold weather, drawn curtains reduce heat loss. Fluorescent tubes requiring no shades cut to one-fifth the energy consumed by incandescent bulbs.

Summary

The prototype home supports solar, wind, water, methane and wood power as energy alternatives. It enables a family, or one person, to build a fully-functioning home-environmental center. It can greatly increase the number who dream of building a home who actually achieve it.

17

green Revolution, misappropriated

he School of Living had used the term "Green Revolution" for nearly thirty years. We were glad for the response, and thrilled at the meaning added to it by intelligent homesteaders, editors, and journalists. We were pleased with the spread of the concepts and practices of an organic green revolution. Pleased—but not entirely satisfied. Who can be satisfied with slow-motion of what is felt to be vital for human welfare as a decentralist revolution amidst wholesale centralization? We continued working for, and welcoming, any evidence of change in the decentralist direction. In the spring of 1969, our treasured term leaped out from headlines in the daily paper:

GREEN REVOLUTION TO FEED STARVING MILLIONS

I read the Baltimore Sun story quickly. Biologist Norman Borlaug of Indiana University was in Mexico, experimenting with improved yields of wheat. Mexico needed grain; wheat would grow in the cooler uplands, but the heads were light with few, light-weight kernels. He crossed native wheat with heavy American strains. Plump heavy heads resulted, but with added difficulties.

The straw was too weak to bear the weight. The plant stems broke and fell—the grain could not be harvested. But with added crossing and more experimenting, Borlaug developed wheat with sturdy straw and heavy heads. Yields in Mexico increased tenfold!

Borlaug developed strains of high-yielding wheat that could grow in India and the Far East. He also brought strains of rice to much higher yields. These new foods would mean new life to the starving millions in the undeveloped countries. This, said the newspaper account, was a "Green Revolution."

"Good!" I thought, and read on. Borlaug and the persons heading this "Green Revolution" were hardly decentralists. The new wheat and rice would be grown in thousand-acre fields; they required lots of water from irrigation. With these new grains were exported huge harvesting machines, tons of chemical fertilizers and sprays to fend off fungi and insects. *This* was a "Green Revolution?"

"Plagiarism, travesty, mis-use of our thirty-year-old term!" I protested to newspapers and the U.S. Department of Agriculture. "Such practices would not really help. In the long run, they will burden the new countries. They were what *our* Green Revolution had rejected three decades ago!" Officials of USDA briefly acknowledged my letters, but no discussion resulted.

Not more than a year later, a different tone appeared in public reports of this "new" green revolution. In April, 1969, scientist C.R. Wharton titled his article in *Foreign Affairs Journal*, "Is The Green Revolution Cornucopia Or Pandora's Box?"

"The green revolution," he said, "is straining investment capital to buy large tracts of land needed for the new program and its big machines. Native skill was not available to handle the machines, nor were there mechanics for repairing their breakdowns. Consequently, harvesters are left to rust in the fields."

Also, harvests were so large that storage, transportation, and marketing facilities were not available. The local people didn't like the taste of the new grains, and wouldn't eat them. Worst of all, landless workers were not getting their share of the "green revolution" prosperity. Riots broke out; fields were burned. In some cities, notably Madras, people were killed. Newspapers all over the world reported the inevitable tragedy that happened in the name of "green revolution."

I was incensed. So were other decentralists and School of Living members, at the misuse of our term. We shot off more letters to editors and agricultural authorities.

DECENTRALISM

"Why," we asked them, "should a term christened in 1940 to mean decentralized agriculture in a decentralist society now be applied to commercial agriculture in Asia and Africa?" "Why, after fifty years of increasing problems with agribusiness in our country should Americans export it under the name of the 'green revolution' to India and Thailand?"

These letters appeared in the *National Observer, Christian Science Monitor, Baltimore Sun*—and in India, *Sarvodaya, Gandhi Marg*, and others. Still, no discussion from the U.S. Department of Agriculture.

In August, 1974, I noted a color-jumbled headline: "Green Revolution Future is Black." This article reported that Borlaug and his green revolution advocates had made a mistake. Mono-cultured, chemically fertilized and sprayed grains were subject to disease.

"The spread of disease by this large-scale mono-crop agriculture could bring about serious worldwide starvation. A whole season's production could be wiped out. The 'green revolution' was a mistake!" Who released this report? None other than the United States Department of Agriculture.

Decentralists and organic farmers could nod our heads in "I told you so." But more dismay overcame us. Wouldn't the discredit, the bad reputation of a false "green revolution," be transferred to our movement?

"Don't fret," Borsodi wrote me. "People will recognize the U.S. Department of Agriculture promoting agribusiness in foreign countries as another fiasco. I doubt if negative meaning will attach to us. The past thirty years have laid a foundation for rethinking our country's wealth and power, and its agriculture along with it. There's ample proof now that only one revolution is green—the one that enriches the soil, that gives people both security and freedom, the one that enhances, not threatens, life. I believe we are on the verge of a real, green, post-industrial and decentralist revolution."

Many events and activities in addition to the ones chronicled in this book confirm that a valid movement was christened in 1940. Its name has withstood abuse. As we move into the 1980s, the cheer rings firmer and stronger, "Long live the Green Revolution!"

18
small community:
bryn gweled, 1939—1980

A visible and viable movement toward creating new "intentional communities," and to maintaining and improving existing villages and small towns, is under way in America. This is to retain and revive some of the simplicity and naturalness of the normal way of living for human beings, following in the footsteps of some of the community-building decentralists mentioned in earlier chapters.

Two 20th Century Americans made a special contribution to the building of community—Ralph Borsodi and Arthur Morgan. Each established an organization through which to build and improve human community—The School of Living, and Community Service, Inc. Both men, and their organizational co-workers, brought standards and resources to add strength and stature to village/community life. Their community goals, methods, places for study-action, and their achievements are part of America's decentralist revolution.

Communities are not casual or impulsive groupings. New communities are willing to observe and study the nature of true community, to instill in them good human relationships, and the new institutional arrangements needed for today's world. The influence of Borsodi and Morgan was to include as well ethical land tenure, just and fair financing, and the use of both individual and cooperative effort with a minimum of legal force, i.e., government. Their communities continue into the 1980s, testimony to their vision and determination.

DECENTRALISM

I describe the community Bryn Gweled, a direct out-growth of Ralph Borsodi's work, and introduce Dr. Arthur E. Morgan and Community Service, Inc., of Yellow Springs, Ohio.

Bryn Gweled Community—Hill of Vision

Bryn Gweled, a community of 77 families totaling 350 persons, still flourishes on the northwest edge of Philadelphia. It is historically tied with the 1933 Dayton Liberty Homesteads, and the influence of Ralph Borsodi on two young teachers there, Georgia Snyder and myself.

Georgia and I were among the Columbia University degree-seekers who "discovered" Ralph Borsodi in 1932. In 1934, Georgia married Herbert Bergstom, and with him, directed Bedford Community Center in Philadelphia's ghetto. I had gone to similar social work in Chicago. But in a few years, our enthusiasm for "club work" and finding jobs for the unemployed was waning. In 1939, I was assisting the Borsodis at the School of Living in Suffern, New York, and the Bergstroms came to visit.

They were entranced with the productive homestead community at Suffern. They immediately wanted to do something similar near Philadelphia. "Where do we begin?" they asked.

"With study and planning," Borsodi replied.

The Bergstroms became enthusiastic. They and co-workers returned many a weekend for reading and discussion on land-site, land-tenure, raising funds, educating candidates on building and homesteading, and related issues. They recruited others, many of them staff persons in the American Friends Service Committee. With them, they formed a Homestead Association, and for two years, they met regularly to study, plan, and prepare for this move to the good life and social change. In 1940, 240 desirable acres became available to them, and a fund was ready for a down payment. Then followed an adventure in community building and living which rewards and stimulates its residents still today.

Bryn Gweled's member-families hold their land in common, but each family has its own lot for its home and buildings. They are Quaker, Catholic, Jewish. Perhaps a third are Blacks. Their membership includes contractors, laborers, lawyers, teachers, engineers, artists, business people, social workers, a tool designer, editors. Most families have children, some having grown, married, and settled down in the community on plots of their own.

Capital funds for the homesteads, including cost of land, roads, installation of utilities, and the community center building, were raised through certificates of indebtedness, bearing 3% interest. Capitalization has always been conservative, and most of the money has come from members themselves. Land assessment paid by each homesteader began at, and remains at, $12 a month. This sum is applied toward a general budget that covers local taxes on land, interest on debts, and repayment of the capital investment.

Bryn Gweled folks handle community chores with "work parties." Each family is expected to give about one day a month in community work. They dug ditches for underground placement of telephone and electric cables. They built a community center and a swimming pool. They maintain trash and poison-plant control with work parties. The economy of getting work done without paid help is important, but more important is the building of unity and the taking on of responsibility for one's own community. They continue to aid each other with tasks such as roofing and gardening. Most families did much of the construction on their own homes. Many families have large gardens, for "homestead" is not merely a euphonious title—homesteads are productive homes.

Of Bryn Gweled's 240 acres, 80 are reserved as common for roads, woods, and recreation. The balance is 81 family leaseholds of about two acres each, leased out for a 99-year renewable term. Each family builds and finances a house suited to its needs, and owns the house, but not the land. If a member takes out a mortgage, Bryn Gweled joins in signing, reserving the right to contribute payment in case a family defaults. Because the land is not owned, and because the house cannot be sold to non-members, Bryn Gweled is attractive only to those who expect to be permanent residents.

The Plot Plan Committee explains to new members and their architect, if any, the few requirements on distances between lot boundaries, structures, well, septic tank systems. Their neighbors are consulted so that major features will be acceptable. Each homeowner plants and develops as he wishes, ranging from natural cover to extensive lawns and landscaping. Though within short distances of each other, no home is visible to its neighbors.

Considerable spontaneous and some organized social life goes on. The community house and playground, tennis court and swimming pool are much used. There are groups who play recorders, sing, square dance, study nature, sew, view films, play and watch sports, or visit around an open fire. The Community and the Children's Committees direct community-wide events—picnics, covered-dish suppers, plays and special occasions.

Bryn Gweled's residents also participate in the civic and social life at the nearby village of Southampton, holding positions on the school board, library board, zoning commission, and in township government. Others participate in Southampton's churches, political and social groups, Boy Scouts, PTA, and Volunteer Fire Company. Bryn Gweled's teenagers edit a popular weekly, *Vox Gweledorum*.

In the 1980s, persons who constitute Bryn Gweled Community are realizing goals set thirty-some years ago. They look on the past with joy, and to the future with anticipation. They do, indeed, warrant their community's name, Bryn Gweled—Welsh for "Hill of Vision."

19
community service inc.:
dr. a.e. morgan

Dr. Arthur E. Morgan lived from 1878 to 1975. His long life, integrity, quality, and diversity of achievement made him an extraordinary decentralist. He is another, who, without a college education, found wisdom from his own search and experience.

Arthur Morgan and his wife, Lucy, and three children (Ernest, Elizabeth and Griscom) lived quietly in Yellow Springs, Ohio. Yet they made of this small town a center for seekers and educators far and near. The Morgans have been unceasingly part of the healthful, simpler, and more real concerns of living, including Arthur Morgan's contribution in several important national projects.

In 1913, a disastrous flood hit Ohio's lower Miami River area. Dayton's central business district was under twelve feet of water, and the lowlands for miles were inundated. Hundreds of people lost their lives, and millions of dollars worth of property was destroyed. Although he was not an engineer, Arthur Morgan had studied, and he had written a book, *The Drainage of the Santa Fe in Arkansas*. He was asked to assess the Dayton situation, and later he was appointed head of the reconstruction of the Miami Valley. He arranged for spanning five small river-valleys converging at Dayton with five huge earth-dams. These dams required earth-moving equal to that in the Panama Canal construction. As a magnificent testimony to Arthur Morgan's success, these five dams still block off the streams into wide-spreading conservancy lakes.

DECENTRALISM

U.S. President Franklin Roosevelt invited Arthur Morgan to take charge of the flood control of the whole Tennessee Valley. The Tennessee Valley Authority was even then a big operation—millions of dollars of government money to spend; thousands of people affected; several thousand employed; stupendous physical and engineering aspects successfully confronted. But the human, the ethical, the relationships among people were a different matter. Arthur Morgan saw his co-workers succumb to dishonesty, chicanery, rivalry, mis-use of funds, and abuse of authority. He deplored the absence of basic integrity.

Reflecting on the need for, causes of, and decline in, the personal character of so many individuals, Arthur Morgan made significant conclusions. In *The Long Road*, he pointed up the cultural roots of immorality. It stems, he said, from modern "specialization"—a lack of diversity, a turning from solving many difficulties in life, especially in youth. He raised questions about the mechanical and scientific complications of the modern world, and the helplessness we face when our telephone or radio is out of order, or when a town needs a new bridge, or when our roses develop a new malady. Morgan preferred a road steering away from specialized doctors, financiers, chemists, educators, etc., to find a culture in something larger, namely, a developed human being. He saw the roots for a human culture in "good homes and small communities." So Morgan left the TVA to return to Yellow Springs, there to devote his life to that small town and other small towns like it.

At this time, Antioch College needed a new president, and the trustees honored Arthur Morgan with the task, although he had no degrees. They conferred on him a doctorate. At Antioch, he initiated the work-study cooperative plan, in which students spend a period studying on the campus, and follow it with a period at work in the larger world.

Dr. Morgan's next step was "to strengthen the small community in America." His family joined him in 1940 to establish Community Service, Inc., to counsel people in developing intentional communities and in improving the nature and quality of existing small towns. With this, of course, he faced the implications of technology, of attitudes, and of philosophical grounds. Griscom Morgan and his wife, Jane, developed their

124

own homestead in the Vale Community, to foster an experimental intentional community with its own mother-taught children's school. Ernest Morgan developed a family-owned business in bookplates, and later, he and his wife assisted in Celo Community, near Burnsville, North Carolina.

Celo is a cooperative land-holding community with title to land in a Homesteaders' Association which leases land to the members. There now are nearly 100 members who have developed a variety of small-scale enterprises—a book-publishing company, a memorial burial society, and the Arthur Morgan School for Children, free of regimentation.

In many ways, Yellow Springs responded to the Morgan influence. Citizens took part in town-planning, not so much to increase the size of their town, as to improve the people's health and well-being, and to improve the town's appearance. A community forest with its now-famous Glen Helen has an outdoor-education center and well-developed trails for nature study. The Fels Laboratory carries on child-care research in Yellow Springs. Many Antioch College students find a model and challenge in their college town.

Griscom and Jane Morgan, plus others, are staff members of Community Service Inc., counselling community builders, publishing books, pamphlets, and a bi-monthly newsletter; holding an annual conference; maintaining an excellent library and book service. Among their 1,000 titles is their own *Guidebook For Intentional Communities*.

"A good community will not be invented, discovered, or 'just grow'," said Dr. Morgan in 1975, when he was 97 years old. "It must be forged from the purpose and quality of the lives of people living in it."

Dr. Morgan was much involved in native-American rights, and worked for years to aid the Seneca Nation in a struggle to retain their treaty-guaranteed lands.

Both Lucy Morgan and Dr. Charles Leuba wrote a biography of Arthur Morgan.

Community Service, Inc., has brought significance to thousands of small communities in America, as well as interpreting their part in the "small, molecular, moral forces" which change cultural patterns.

20
the community land trust

As Ralph Borsodi knew so well, a chief hurdle to wide-spread and rapid moving of families to country homesteads (as well as other kinds of decentralization) is the rising cost of land. Twice, as prime-mover in homesteading communities, he had initiated a new form of land tenure. It was known as the 999-lease in Dayton's Liberty Homesteads, and the indenture plan in the School of Living Bayard Lane Community. Similar programs were both necessary and anticipated, if decentralization were to proceed noticeably.

In Borsodi's lifetime, a new land tenure surfaced again in 1966 through the cooperation with another decentralist, Robert Swann. During World War II, Swann was in prison for conscientious objection to war. In a group of COs, there was study of the newly-forming decentralist movement. They followed a study-course developed by Ralph Templin, then director of the School of Living. Their texts were Arthur Morgan's *The Small Community* and Borsodi's *Flight From The City*, *This Ugly Civilization*, and *Prosperity and Security*. Outstanding in this study was the way the School of Living communities held land in trust, each member-family leasing from the community, and not selling the land as private property. This impressed Robert Swann, and since 1945, occupied a large place in his thinking.

In the late 1940s, Robert married, and he and his wife, Marjorie, both were active in the Peace and Civil Rights Movements in picketing, civil disobedience, and resisting U.S. engagement in the Korean and Vietnam Wars. Both of them saw decentralism consistent with, and necessary to, non-violence, as perceived by M.K. Gandhi.

126

Robert Swann was carpenter, designer, and builder of houses. In two cooperatively-owned enterprises (in his hometown, Yellow Springs, Ohio, and Kalamazoo, Michigan) he learned how crucial land values are to low-cost housing. In 1956, he joined Morris Milgram in the first racially-integrated housing in Philadelphia. Again, he saw how much land- or site-value hampers successful housing. More time and money are spent by builders in the United States locating suitable land than on actual supervision and building.

Both Marjorie and Robert realized that speculation in land and natural resources is a root cause of a great deal of injustice, and therefore, violence. For their life-base, the Swanns developed in 1960 the CNVA Farm (Committee For Non-Violent Action) in Voluntown, Connecticut. They organized it as a trust, with community-held land. They urged the peace movement to augment picketing, protest marches, boycotts, and civil disobedience, with decentralization and removing land from private exploitation and profit.

Most non-violent activists, according to Swann, tended either toward socialism or anarchism, neither well-defined nor articulated. Most pacifists disclaimed socialism as practiced, but seemed to find no other term to describe their essentially humanistic economics and politics. Swann found Borsodi's thinking and action rigorous in examining all aspects of life. In his view, Borsodi's courage in maintaining that economics must deal with moral issues, refreshingly contrasted with most well-known economists. He decided to tie in with Borsodi.

In the early 1960s, Robert Swann was working in the Civil Rights Movement in the U.S. South—rebuilding burned-out churches in Mississippi after the "hot summer" of 1964. Seeing the landlessness, the helplessness of the Black population, Swann saw their need to get on land of their own. He learned that Ralph Borsodi had just returned from four years in India, and had similar ideas for *world* development.

In India, Borsodi had had long conferences with leaders of the Gramdan movement, particularly Jayapakash Narayan, who, as follower of Vinoba Bhave, had become a prominent leader. In 1953, Narayan gave up his post in the cabinet (and probably his prime ministership) to join

DECENTRALISM

Vinoba Bhave, then walking through the villages of India, asking for land to be put in trusteeship under the Gramdan village control of all land. When Borsodi met with Narayan in 1966, the Gramdan movement included thousands of villages, affecting the lives of millions of people.

Borsodi recognized Gramdan as similar to the hopes and plans he had presented in Dayton and the Suffern School of Living communities. In Gramdan and Narayan were a power and a force which needed to spread around the world as an alternative to the centralist methods of communism, socialism, and state capitalism. In India, the Gandhian heritage and organization provided Narayan a following of millions. In America, the pseudo-economics of Keynesianism and the "affluent society" made serious consideration of Borsodi's ideas difficult.

Ralph Borsodi and Robert Swann joined forces. The two men put their energies into forming a non-national agency to revitalize rural areas throughout the world. In 1967, with the help of Dr. R.E. Dewey of the University of New Hampshire, Dr. Gordon Lameyer of Bradford College, and myself, Mildred Loomis, from the School of Living, the International Independence Institute was launched for this purpose.

Persons from any part of the world may become members, depositors, and investors in the International Independence Institute (III), a non-profit cooperative registered in Luxembourg, whose main purpose is to teach, sponsor, and assist the formation of Community Land Trusts.

The Community Land Trust is a legal entity, a quasi-public body, chartered under state laws to hold land in stewardship for all mankind. It is administered by a board of trustees, some of whom may live on trust land, but (to insure wider interest and community responsibility) 50% of the trustees do not. The Community Land Trust implements holding of land for the common good; it is not primarily concerned with common ownership.

The trustees of a trust secure land by gift or purchase, and then declare (and hold) it nonsalable. They arrange trust agreements (contracts) with those who will use the land constructively, and who, instead of a purchase price, pay an annual rental to the trust equal to the economic rent of the land. Out of this fund, the Trust pays the county and state land

128

taxes. Land-users build, own, sell, and use the buildings and labor products on the land as their own private property.

Returned to the South with land-trust agreements, Robert Swann found Southern leaders understanding and approving. He met Slater King, a relative of Martin Luther King; a real-estate dealer; and a civil-rights leader in Albany, Georgia. In spite of discrimination problems, Slater King was helping the poor get land of their own. He saw the land trust as an equitable and just method of holding land, and a way by which Blacks could not be thrown off their land because of ignorance or white chicanery.

Slater King and Swann arranged for a group of Southern leaders to go to Israel to study the Jewish National Fund, one of the oldest, largest, and most successful land-trust arrangements in the world. Israelis had held land in trust since 1890, when the first Zionists came to Palestine and bought land from absentee Arab landlords.

Heads of seven influential groups in the South who made the trip to Israel included Faye Bennett, executive secretary of the National Sharecroppers Fund; Slater and Marion King; Charles Sherrod, officer of the Student Nonviolent Coordinating Committee (SNCC); Albert Turner of the Southern Christian Leadership Council; Lewis Black of the Southwest Alabama Farmers' Cooperative Association; Leonard Smith, a regional director of the National Sharecroppers' Fund; and Swann, as head of the international Independence Institute. That such a group of leaders could be assembled in a short time indicates the welcome for the trust idea, and at the same time, each group constituted avenues for effective spreading of the idea.

From their study and tour of Israel, these leaders recommended the land trust to their constituents. Conferences were held in several places, and action taken in 1969. In the spring, New Communities, Inc., was formed to operate as III's first land trust. An option was taken on 4,800 acres near Albany, Georgia.

Financing (over $1,000,000) came from trust members, as well as from religious denominations, governmental and educational groups. Officers and members of New Communities Trust were Blacks and whites, as were applicants for family homesteads on trust acreage. The plan combined private homesteads on some land and cooperative farming of other areas—an adaptation of the *moshave* in Israel. Families lived on their 5-acre homesteads via lifetime lease of the land from New Communities, and held private ownership of improvements. They could earn additional money by cooperative farming on some of the trust acres. Other earnings in the cooperative went to develop the entire community.

The significance of the International Independence Institute lay not only in achieving the nearly 5,000-acre Albany trust, but in being an agency for continuing such projects elsewhere. Here, for the first time in U.S. history, was an open, voluntary agency, one of whose primary purposes was to achieve land reform in the framework of liberty and security, stemming from America's unique economist-philosophers, Henry George and Ralph Borsodi.

Word spread of the Independence Institute and its work. Calls came from other trust developers for III's help and supervision. To serve all inquirers, in 1972 the III published a handbook, *The Community Land Trust: A Guide To A New Land Tenure In America*. Part I defines the concept and discusses its application and political dimensions. Foreign and American models in actual use are described, and the process of incorporation outlined. Part II deals with the organization, structure, land selection, financing, land use, and social planning. Included are how to determine rent, the matters of taxation, zoning and codes, as well as duplicates of actual lease contracts in use. Included are replicas of eight actual land-trust contracts: the early School of Living "Indenture for the Possession of land," "Contract for Lease of a Farm under the Jewish National Fund," the Voluntown Peace Trust, the New Communities Trust, incorporation and by-laws of Bryn Gweled Homesteads, and others.

Robert Swann traveled widely by invitation and to conferences on trust action—to Europe, South America, Mexico. Successful land trusts formed in Puerto Rico and Mexico provide alternative land systems to the owner/tenant relationship on sugar, coffee, and cotton plantations.

In the United States, a growing youth movement in the 1970s was seeking "community on the land." Many young people, generally ethical and non-materialistic in outlook, welcomed the justice implicit in the community land trust. Counter-culture media swept the term into prominence and it is now much discussed.

Special journals appeared to espouse land reform and give space to community land trusts. Outstanding are *The Maine Land Advocate* (Orono, Maine) and *People and Land* (San Francisco). Among the 100 community land trusts operating in the United States are Northern California Trust, a function of a Coalition for Land Reform; the Evergreen Land Trust in Washington state; and the Sam Ely Trust (Brunswick, Maine) working toward a regional trust to include much of the land in Maine. In Madison, Wisconsin, a School of Living member, Bruce Allison, is working with a group to put a large area of southeastern Wisconsin into a regional land trust.

In 1976, the School of Living incorporated into a trust the land of some of its centers. Increasing its own trust and guiding other community land trust developers is a major emphasis of the School of Living.

The American Dream—family maintenance and economic freedom—cannot be achieved in the milieu of high land costs, mortgages, foreclosures, and taxes. Individuals and families, by themselves, are tied to the treadmill of working and saving, only to see their resources dwindle because of inflation, high cost of food and transportation, and especially the increasing cost of living space through rent and price of land.

At a time when human use and mis-use of the earth is a matter of vital concern, the Community Land Trust not only affords a ready instrument for the protection of land and the husbanding of its resources for future generations, but it also enables persons to effect significant changes in social policy in the face of apparent governmental lethargy.

As a way to lessen exploitation and to lower and eliminate the cost of land, the Community Land Trust is an urgent and significant aspect of the Decentralist Revolution.

21

constant currency

he Possessional Problem of Living has a second part, besides land. Eliminating monopolies in credit, money, banking, and the issuing and redeeming of currency affects the decentralization of America. Ever-increasing inflation and rising prices of goods plague the average American family, both causing, and resulting from, unbalanced federal budgets and the government's printing of money.

One government administration follows another counseling citizen conservation of energy, while the government continues a dishonest money system and initiates programs which waste energy and increase the federal deficit and unbalance the budget. So common is the unbalanced federal budget that it's come to be accepted as The American Way— "We've always had one."

Actually, an unbalanced annual budget of the U.S. Government did not appear until 1950. In 1800, the federal budget was $11 million; the tax-burden was $2 per individual, and the national debt (after a long Revolutionary War) was $83 million. But the *annual* federal budget was in surplus. By 1900, the national budget had soared to $521 million, the tax burden per person to $7, and the total national debt to $1.4 billion. But still, the budget was in surplus.

It took a century and a half (from 1800 to 1950) for the national government to accumulate its first $250 billion of debt. In the next three decades (1950–1980), the U.S. Treasury will have more than tripled the level of debt accumulated in the previous 150 years. In the fiscal year ended October, 1977, the budget outlay was $422 billion; the per capita tax burden a staggering $2,000; with the nation's debt headed toward $750 billion, and the budget in deficit almost $70 billion! This rising level of treasury debt represents only the accumulated cash deficit of the government in Washington. It does not include the debt of state or municipal governments (or the various agencies within them, like sewer authorities and school boards).

The federal budget deficit is simply what politicians in Washington spend over and above the taxes they collect from citizens in cash. In three years (1975–78), the U.S. Government increased its debt more than in the three decades 1945 to 1975—years of the Korean War, the Vietnam catastrophe, and the Great Society's New Frontier.

To a decentralist revolutionary, the national debt represents loss of national independence, just as a personal growing debt to one's banker suggests increasing dependence on him. In 1968, the interest on the national debt was $15.4 billion; in January, 1977, it had risen to $40.7 billion. The interest on the federal debt is now almost 40% of all money spent on the Western world's largest military establishment—and that is larger than the annual cost of all schools, colleges, and education.

Rich American citizens own much of the national debt in the form of treasury bonds and government securities. Middle-class Americans are paying interest to them. Serious as that is, it is worse that the foreign ownership of the U.S. Government debt has risen sharply. In December, 1939, it was $200,000; in December, 1976, over $100 billion! Eighty percent of this debt is readily marketable whenever those foreign governments and individuals choose to cash it in. On this international level, governments and empires are made and broken! This process of foreign indebtedness accompanied the disintegration of the British Empire.

In 1977, the International Monetary Fund again rescued the collapsing British pound with a $4 billion loan. The pound sterling collapsed because Arab oil sheiks and other foreigners decided to sell their large holdings of British government debt securities for dollars, marks, yen, and Swiss francs. A century of British budgetary deficits had caused this loss of confidence. A once-stable British Empire was prostrate before former vassals and the Middle Eastern oil bankers, now the owners of the British national debt.

The inescapable point is that America too is losing her independence to foreign bankers. The hard-earned taxes of U.S. working people are being transferred to foreigners in order to pay the interest and principal on the national debt which foreigners own. We are transferring an even larger part of this total debt itself to foreign creditors. We are mortgaging the Republic to strangers and governments over whom we have no control, and of whose loyalty we can never be sure. The pervasive and irresponsible momentum of federal government expenditures is to make the U.S. Republic an increasingly insolvent and illogical debtor.

The course of any debt-ridden individual or institution is loss of personal freedom. When a national government spends more than it taxes (and borrows from its own rich citizens and rich foreigners), that nation not only impoverishes its working people by taxing them to pay the interest, but such a nation will, in the end, forfeit its sovereignty.

Debt-ridden citizens increasingly lose their freedom and their self-esteem. Debt-ridden nations lose their sovereign independence.

An Honest Money System: Constant Currency

Ralph Borsodi had long been aware of the complex, serious financial difficulties in the United States and the world. He understood not only the operations of the existing money system (relatively rare even among public leaders, not to mention the average citizen). Borsodi was confident of the fundamentals of an honest, stable system of banking and currency. He had outlined and called for such a plan in 1943 in his Inflation Is Coming!

Inflation did come, not as rapidly nor to a crescendo of run-away proportions as Borsodi had predicted. Such dramatic inflation was forestalled by government acceptance of Keynesian-controlled inflation, with increasing government regulation of prices and the market. Americans have escaped (so far) the catastrophe of runaway inflation, but at increasing loss of liberty.

Ralph Borsodi could not believe that liberty-loving Americans would tolerate such extensive government controls of industry and prices as they did in the quarter-century following 1943.

With alarm, Borsodi watched the world's financial crisis deepen in 1972. Troubled, but not surprised, he read in the newspapers in March, 1972, that U.S. President Nixon had devalued the dollar. Theft and robbery, Borsodi called it—the reduction of value in the people's savings by 25%, a regressive tax levied on people without their participation, understanding, or consent.

What should he do? Decentralist revolutionary that he was, Borsodi believed that government has no place in administering or controlling money. Government should only set standards for money—as it does in weights and measures. Government should not operate banks, nor issue money. Banks should be cooperatives of depositors. Commercial banks should issue money, backed by actual goods going to market.

Borsodi could write another book—repeat what he had presented in earlier books, elaborate the cause and cure of inflation. But the world has had enough words—plenty of books on money reform have been read, set aside, and forgotten. "What is needed," he decided, "is an experiment, a *demonstration* of an honest, stable, currency. Real people in an actual community could and should print and circulate their own money—operating their own banking system."

Ralph Borsodi realized the challenge of such a proposal; he foresaw the hurdles and obstacles. "Money reform is the most difficult of all necessary social changes," he admitted, "but second only to land reform is urgency for a decentralist revolution."

Borsodi decided to act—to start a new, people's money, to experiment in his own hometown and state. Since 1974, Borsodi had lived in Exeter, New Hampshire, a typical New England small town, a good place (utopia) of some 2500 people. He explained his plan to Exeter bankers and some businessmen. They were willing to cooperate. Several hundred friends and neighbors became investors in a new non-profit cooperative corporation, the International Foundation for Independence, to operate an ethical money system, as the International Institute for Independence had brought an ethical land system into being.

The International Foundation for Independence was different—it was cooperative and voluntary, instead of governmental; it was world-wide, registered in Luxembourg; it would issue money with a new standard and backing. Certainly its money would not be tied to government debt. It would not be based on one commodity—gold—as some money experts proposed. (History had proved that the price of gold is too fluctuating, dependent as it is on the uncertain discovery and supply of gold.)

The new money would be based on, and backed by, a select number, or "basket" of 30 staple commodities, such as silver, gold, aluminum, zinc, lead, tin, wheat, oats, rye, soybeans, sugar, peanuts, rice, coal, iron, oil, etc. Check-like notes were printed in various amounts, called "Constants." Each Constant was equal to 20 cents; five Constants equaled one dollar. Quantities of commodities in which the Constant could be redeemed were listed on the back of each one.

This particular "basket" of commodities represents an accurate cross-section of the basic elements of the world economy. Since inflation, almost by definition, expresses itself as a rise in the average prices of such commodities, a currency based on holdings of such commodities would have a stable constant relationship to them, and thus to prices in general.

While the price of one or two commodities might drop in the world market, it is not likely that all would. Thus a fluctuation *within* the basket would not seriously affect the *whole*. The issuing corporation, IFI, is obligated to maintain one such "basket" of commodity holdings for each 50,000 Constants in circulation, and to redeem them in kind, on demand. Thus, unlike the U.S. Government, the IFI could not just print more Constants than they had commodities. Thus, its currency was not inflatable.

Robert Swann assumed the directorship of the International Foundation for Independence to take the Constant into a larger-than-local test. He would supervise the nature and weight of the commodities in the "basket" or Index which backed the money; he would assemble a fund of capital large enough to move into the commodities "futures" market.

This "futures" market of staple commodities on the international level would involve the purchase and sale on the same day, to take advantage of differing price levels at different spots on the globe. Known as "arbitrage," this buying and selling on the same day would not be speculation. Speculation is the deliberate holding of goods off the market for some time, in anticipation of a price rise. Arbitrage would involve the buying of wheat in Egypt, and selling it at a fraction of a cent more per pound in London, on the same day. In this way, arbitrage would facilitate trade, rather than hinder it, as does speculation.

The experiment with Constants operated for more than a year in Exeter, New ampshire., and its surrounding territory. It was reported and described in *Forbes Magazine*, *Business Week*, *Financial World*, the *Boston Globe*, and other newspapers. It demonstrated the structure and operation of an honest money system. It developed a fund for loaning to small-scale enterprises, particularly in the Third World, at reasonable (5, 7, and 10%) rates of interest. (In many Third World countries, particularly India, money lenders charge 33% to 50% interest on loaned money.)

This effort at an ethical money system continues into the future under a new name—The International Community Development Fund. Emphasis is on loaning, and on building a fund of adequate size to support the launching of the Constant on a world scale.

A second type of reform to which decentralists give some support is demurrage money, announced by Silvio Gesell in the 19th century. Money represents commodities; commodities (grain, lumber, metals) deteriorate with rust, moths, and age; owners of commodities thus suffer a loss. Said Gesell, "Ownership of money should bear a similar loss, cost, or depreciation."

He suggested that money hoarded or not circulating in the market in trade should bear a monthly tax or demurrage. Thus money would not be held out of use (for collecting interest); it would circulate, and the market would have adequate media to transfer goods.

Prior to World War II, demurrage money was practiced in Woergel, Germany, and in a number of Austrian cities. It circulated and stabilized currency while other regions with conventional money succumbed to ca-

DECENTRALISM

lamitous inflation. But since demurrage money was prohibited and out-
lawed by Hitler, its practice was short-lived.

Another improvement over the debt-debased money promoted today is "gold-standard" money. While gold-based money suffers the un-
certainty of the gold supply in the world, it is superior to government
printing-press money, debt-based currency. Among those teaching and
supporting gold-backed money are the Foundation for Economic Education, Great Barrington, Massachusetts; Murray Rothbard, author of
Power and Market and *Government and The Economy*; Dr. Milton Friedman,
professor of history in the University of Chicago, and author of *Monetary
History of the United States*.

22

Rural Revival on the Way: Robert Rodale

One of the prime goals of life in this self-centered age is to be where the action is—or where you think it's going to be when you get ready to claim a piece of it. For about 150 years, the action has largely been in big cities. Generations of young people have headed to New York, Chicago, San Francisco, seeking their fortune, with a certainty of finding it. All that was needed was a reasonably good education, a desire to work (usually not too hard), and some luck.

"How are you going to keep them down on the farm," the saying went, and it sure did have an impact on the population distribution of this country. The cities kept expanding and growing; rural regions were drained of their best and brightest youth. The most admired and successful people lived in the largest cities—making their homes in large apartment buildings as far removed as possible from the earth, the cackling of hens, and the aroma of rotting manure.

In 1970, many of these city folks woke up and realized they were in a kind of prison. Sure, they still liked the bright lights, the plays, the restaurants, and their friends. And they liked the big money they were making. But often, they were afraid to walk the streets at night, and sometimes in the daytime, too. In fact, from a multitude of directions, they saw the cities begin to decline and even degenerate—trapping their occupants in a most unpleasant web of human and physical decay. The prisoners began to seek means of escape.

DECENTRALISM

Of course, many of the affluent city people had been heading for the suburbs and the exurbs for the past 30 years. But now, given the magnitude of city problems, even that doesn't seem quite far enough from the declining core of places like New York. The problems of the central cities have followed into the suburbs. Many suburbs have become like cities, with crowding, high rise apartments and offices, high taxes, rising crime rates and similar annoyances.

So, starting only a couple of years ago, the movement of people from country to city stopped. Then to the surprise of experts in people-watching and head-counting, the tide of population growth swung the other way, reversing a historically-entrenched trend. The fastest population growth at least in percentage points was in some of the most remote and formerly unattractive areas.

One of the first government experts to analyze and comment on the rural growth trend was Calvin L. Beale, a program leader of the Population Studies Group of the U.S. Department of Agriculture. In January, 1975, writing in the *Journal of Soil and Water Conservation*, he pointed out surprising facts about this new rural growth. What had been looked on as prime places to leave were now experiencing the greatest growth in population.

Four areas now attracting the highest percentage of growth are:

1. Eastern Kentucky and the Southern Appalachian Region. The energy situation plays an important role here. Coal areas are again becoming islands of prosperity, but that's not the whole story.

2. The Rocky Mountain Area from Northern Idaho down to Southern New Mexico is growing in people at the rate of 7% a year.

3. Upper Michigan and the whole upper Great Lakes region is growing at about 8% a year.

4. The Ozark-Ouchita Mountain area, from northern Texas through Oklahoma, is the fastest-growing of all large geographical areas of the U.S., exceeding 9.4%.

Some rural areas are not experiencing growth, such as the Great Plains, but who is to say their people magnetism is not more than a few years away? Beale describes the population shifts as "simply incredible."

"We knew this trend was coming, but the speed and extent have been astonishing. In three years we've already had as much movement from urban to rural as I thought we'd have during the entire 1970s." He claims the trend is going to continue and very likely accelerate.

Why is this historic movement of people happening? I think it's obvious that the basic reason is that people have found out that they can't live at desirable levels of satisfaction in areas of high population density. Sure, all of us enjoy having friends, and we want to be near them. But we are finding that people in large masses, crammed together with their possessions and with the desire to live life at a fast pace, can be a real burden to one another. We put up with those people-problems for a time, and then we want out—to where there is peace and quiet and a chance to create self-sufficiency by growing some of our own food and generating some of our own power. Beale and other population experts point to other reasons for the new rural growth, but I think they are all spin-offs of the desire to put distance between one's self and the mob, and to generate self-sufficiency.

For example, outdoor recreation has boomed. Millions are out hiking, climbing mountains, boating, bird-watching and simply looking for uncrowded places to commune with nature. That urge to get outdoors has led to developing resort, recreation, and retirement areas in far-rural sections. They offer job opportunities. Industrial job opportunities are growing in small towns and rural areas. Businesses are finding the problems in cities a threat to their well-being, and are moving out to greener pastures. Naturally, people move with them. Improved transportation and lower costs of operation are increasing profit possibilities for businesses in non-metropolitan areas.

The tightening energy situation is also changing the shape of our society in several ways. The boom of Appalachia is just one example. Energy from coal mined in the Rocky Mountain states costs about 25 cents per million BTUs, while the imported oil in the coastal states costs about $2 per million BTUs.

"It seems evident," says editor P.H. Abelson of *Science*, "that coastal areas of this country are entering an era in which they will be handicapped relative to some interior states." Coastal states, particularly in the Northeast, harbor the biggest group of large cities in America.

Perhaps the most important force in the new rural migration is the fundamental desire to return to the land. Beale cites that as his final reason for the new rural growth. "There is a significant change in attitudes and values about where and how people want to live," he says. Closeness to the earth and the ability to produce much of one's own food is now valued more highly than the excitement and convenience of cities. Only on the land can true self-sufficiency be aimed for. There is a new willingness to accept the hard work and long hours of small-scale farming, because of the enormous rewards in independence and security.

True, in terms of total numbers, we are talking about a migration of a relatively small portion of the population. But I'm convinced that this recent intensified movement, first, it is just starting. After 150 years of being drained of the best minds and bodies, our rural places are now getting them back. And far more are on the way. The impact of this movement which has already been observed is but a tiny sample of what will be seen in the future.

Second, the people returning to the land today are far different than those who left. They are more mature, better-educated and financed, and more determined to build something good for themselves with their own labor. Having tasted the "delights" of the cities, they now see the enormous potential of America's rural regions to be their real promised land.

Third and most important, the new rural migrants are positioning themselves to be the primary beneficiaries of the future scientific and technological developments that will be of the most help to mankind, and here are my reasons for this claim.

The Industrial Revolution and most of the technological "miracles" of the past century have almost all been made possible by cheap energy. Those who developed all the tools of modern life—from automobiles and jet planes to pesticides, miracle drugs, and convenience foods—almost never had to consider the energy cost of their creations. In almost every case, these inventions did their tasks by means of enormously increased consumption of energy.

Now, the age of cheap energy is over, so scientific development work is being redirected toward conservation and use of renewable energy sources like sun, wind, biomass (the farm wood lot) and water power. This movement is building rapidly as is the rural migration trend, and the people who are already situated on the land are in an ideal (and possibly the only) position to reap the benefits.

By comparison, those scientific and technological changes that will affect the lives of city people in the future will be largely negative, not beneficial. To solve major urban problems like crime and general social decay, cities will become more sophisticated technological prisons. City people will be watched more carefully by closed-circuit television, more efficiently monitored within their apartments. Food, information, entertainment and other services will be brought to them by "improved" technological means. Converting cities into technological prisons will be the only means to maintain them in operating order so that the needed functions of central government and high-level business directions can be carried on.

Rural people, though, can look forward to these positive results of future technological advance:

1. Country people will control enough access to free energy—sun, wind and water—to make alternate energy sources work effectively. Intensive scientific effort will be directed in these areas to yield results for small-scale application, i.e., ideal for use on rural homesteads and small farms.

2. Biomass also offers unique and fruitful areas for energy development. Many swampy, hilly, and other areas not suitable for large-scale farming are ideal to produce plant life that can be converted directly to energy. Although they don't plan to, rural homesteaders often settle on land well-suited for future biomass production. Scientists are cranking up to tap this source of energy in new ways.

3. One of the richest barely-tapped natural resources is nitrogen in the air, available in almost inexhaustible amounts. Current amounts of extracting require large amounts of oil, gas, or other energy, to function. Gardeners and farmers will soon be able to tap this resource using biologi-

cal nitrogen-fixing methods now being discovered and improved by scientists around the world.

4. Improved electronic technology, which in a gentle way will imprison city people in their apartments, but will help rural homesteaders and farmers stay in touch with the world. While retaining freedom of movement and the pleasures of working in the open air, rural people will have access to the best in education and entertainment.

5. Future health discoveries will make rural life look far better in the future than it seems now. The detrimental effects, both physical and social, of urban pollution, are just beginning to be appreciated. Hard proof of the threats to life and human efficiency of the thousands of synthetic chemicals and pollutants harbored in cities is just beginning to come to light. Why wait ten years for your doctor to tell you to take yourself and your children into an unpolluted area when you can do that now?

6. The autonomous house, the true self-sufficient homestead, will no doubt be possible to build on a sizeable piece of land—in an area far removed from high taxes, high-cost land, polluted water and smog. New developments in building materials and techniques will make the autonomous house easier to build and economically practical.

Yes, there is a rural renaissance under way, and once it gives birth to a new American culture, our country will never be the same again.

23
evolving persons
create mutual society

Decentralists are moving into the 1980s with optimism.

Yet there are serious problems to face. What about the economic and political roots of injustice and oppression? Why is such a high percentage of adults, particularly among minority groups, unable to find employment? Why inflation and rising prices? Prices of land per acre were never higher; neither have taxes per capita been exceeded. And government bureaucracy—in 1920 there were 158 Federal agencies—now there are 17,000.

In addition to changes which must be made in "the system," we know that individuals must change—that we as human beings must evolve into the kind of human beings which we say is ideal, not the kind which the society of the Twentieth Century has generally produced.

An articulate but relatively unpublished voice for evolving humanity is that of Don Werkheiser, former editor of *Journal of Human Relations*. He is putting between covers of three books the result of three decades of observation, study, and experience. His is a thorough analysis of modern exploitative authoritarian relationships, with solutions and suggestions for a "society of mutualism."

As a young man, Werkheiser was critical of both education and modern business, for both, he felt, transgressed his concept of freedom as a primary human need. He chose to earn his living as a carpenter. His concern for liberty led to his friendship with two outstanding libertarian thinkers and writers—Dr. Theodore Schroeder and Laurence Labadie.

Dr. Schroeder has developed theories of evolutionary psychology and the scientific maturing of human emotions. His prolific writings describing the emotional compulsion resulting in dominance/submission and love/hate helped interpret the behavior of power-seeking politicians and monopoly industrialists.

Laurence Labadie, son of Detroit's gentle anarchist of the 1900s, Joe Labadie (secretary to Benjamin Tucker), was heir to the books and writings of Josiah Warren, Stephen Pearl Andrews, Lysander Spooner, and Benjamin Tucker. In association with Labadie, Werkheiser had contact with one of America's ablest interpreters of the early challengers of America's monopoly system.

Werkheiser came to the Lane's End School of Living in the late 1950s, where he assisted in editing and writing the School's journal, *A Way Out*. His discussions there with Laurence Labadie and Ralph Borsodi, who also visited from time to time, were long and deep. He heard me speak of Henry George, and John Loomis spoke of Lafollette's "progressivism." On one point we all agreed: that the generally-accepted economic and political patterns were operating primarily for the benefit of, and under the control of, certain beneficiaries, to the disadvantage of other persons.

Don Werkheiser's writings call this condition "Single Convenience Relationships." Any organism, including a human being, acts in such a way that favorable consequences occur. The producing action thus is reinforced. This is "single-convenience," for the effect on other things or beings is not considered. If this unilateral condition becomes conscious and is pursued successfully in human relationships, one is subordinate to the convenience of the other. The superordinate operates at his own discretion, with his own reinforcing imperatives, to produce those results most favorable to himself. The subordinate does not—he may be excluded, exploited, oppressed, denied, or used according to the convenience of the superordinate. This means that one person is the instrument of the other, and this is the same whether it occurs in a democratic or a totalitarian society.

Werkheiser shows that modern Western society is single-convenience related, and "Single-Option Relationships"—or SOR for short—predominate.

The task of all persons of goodwill, we felt at Lane's End, was to change a society so that each person freely decided his involvement with others. John Loomis and I regarded land monopoly as the starkest evidence of Single-Option Relationships. Labadie and Werkheiser insisted it was banking/money. Ralph Borsodi said both and even others were equally SOR.

What was needed, Werkheiser said, was to create "Mutual-Option Relationships" (MOR). From 1955-1965, these ideas appeared in *Green Revolution*, as well as ideas of Leonard Krimmerman, Murray Rothbard, Murray Bookchin, and Ed Opitz.

In SOR society, authority is mandatory. In a MOR society, authority is advisory—advice can be accepted or rejected. It is important to distinguish between these two styles, rather than rejecting all authority *per se*, Werkheiser points out.

The same is true of the concept of "order." SOR order is external regulation imposed upon others; MOR order is self-regulated direction from within. On human rights: in SOR societies, human rights are permissions of political superiors extended to political inferiors, whereas MOR societies determine human rights by mutual agreement of free people in equal association.

In "Law," too, it is necessary to distinguish between SOR and MOR situations. Single-Option Relationships have political superiors formulating law for political inferiors. Mutual-Option law is formulated by political equals. The U.S. Constitution is an example of SOR law, but the Bill of Rights is one of MOR law. Thus there is a contradiction in the fundamental law of the land. The result is a chaos of arbitrary (SOR) rule imposed in the name of (MOR) democratic law.

"Property" is another concept which becomes pro-human or anti-human depending upon whether the society is SOR or MOR. The essence of property is exclusion, but exclusion can be secured by agreement (MOR) or by might (SOR).

147

DECENTRALISM

In Western Civilization, property is SOR-oriented, and millions of human beings are denied free and equal access to the primary resources of the earth.

Werkheiser believes that to eliminate social problems arising from Single-Option Relationships, human beings must evolve and move toward Mutual-Option. This will happen as humans analyze their situation, reassert individual integrity, emerge from the mass and take action individually and in voluntary groups to improve their relationships.

Werkheiser believes human potential will not be realized until a MOR society is re-achieved. He notes that just as the potential of chimpanzees was not suspected until they were studied in their natural habitat, so the full potential of human beings cannot be apprehended until they live in *their* natural habitat—a mutual-operating society.

He outlines a maturing process through which people outgrow living "by and for their feelings as ends in themselves." Many factors augur hope. Energetic, healthful adults on more and more family homesteads, with a clear concept of a mutual society, can evolve and mature to give promise that in the continuing struggle between Liberty and Authority, decentralism will continue and one day will predominate.

24
cuRReNt actívíty
of ɔeceNtʀaLíst gʀoups

In this purposefully brief scanning of America's decentralist groups, we have seen that throughout our history, some citizens have always been dissidents to authority, and revolutionaries of freedom. Twice in the struggle, when the forces of Authority became oppressive and threatened Liberty, alert defenders stirred support and won a Revolution—the Revolution of Independence and the Civil War.

To some degree, each of these confrontations held Tyranny at bay. But not fully. Each of these revolutions had economic roots, and since these were left essentially untouched, the Revolution's successes were less than complete. Even when free from British monarchs, and when Blacks were no more subject to the monstrous custom of buying and selling, the struggle in America for physical survival pushed some people to subsistence level and below.

The third Revolution—the industrial revolution via steam power, electricity and untold technological wizardry—was to change that situation. From unlimited production of goods, and wealth flowing everywhere, poverty would soon be conquered. America, the land of the free, with endless resources, became the Melting Pot of the world. But by 1930, America had organized life and activity in six ugly Centralizations that more stridently than ever set the haves against the have-nots—centralization in factory production, concentrated ownership, corporate control, standardized education, huge cities and federal bureaucracy.

DECENTRALISM

Leaders appeared and groups organized for America's fourth Revolution—the Decentralist Revolution—to undo, by persuasion and education, those Centralizations. Decentralists would create a truly free human society, suitable for the growth and development of every person. Some of the efforts of America's early individualist-anarchists, Georgists, cooperators and decentralists have been recorded. Some current activities and challenges are added here.

Anarchists and Mutualists:
In addition to the Labadie-Werkheiser contributions to modern anarchist thought, two intrepid souls in this value system are noteworthy. As a Catholic Worker, Ammon Hennacy's life (deceased 1965) verified his book title, *The One Man Revolution*. Paul Goodman's (deceased 1972) versatility as a community planner, humanitarian, friend of youth and intelligent non-statist, is reflected in his own record, *Communitas* and in *Growing Up Absurd*. Fortunately, biographies of these two men are available for study of their diverse and courageous activities.

Dr. Leonard Krimmerman of the University of Louisiana has written *Patterns of Anarchy*; and Dr. James J. Martin of the University of Colorado at Colorado Springs wrote *Men Against the State* in 1952 and *Revisionist Viewpoint* in 1960. In 1979 Martin published *Laurance Labadie's Essays*. Since Murray Bookchin's *Evolution of Radical Thought* was published in *Green Revolution* in 1962, he has issued *The Limits of The City* and other works.

For more than thirty years, Dorothy Day has reported on essentially anarchist experiences in the *Catholic Worker*, and maintained a center for material and spiritual help among the destitute. Similar Houses of Hospitality have been developed in other large cities, and two young disciples, Chuck Smith and Sandy Adams are editing *The Mountain Call* from their Catholic Worker Farm near Spencer, West Virginia.

For years, M. Arnoni edited *Minority of One* in England, and was succeeded by *Minus One* by S. F. Parker, to be followed by John Patworth and Satish Kumar editing *Resurgence*, (Pentre Ifan, Felindre, Crymch, Wales) now in its eighth year.

Libertarians:

Somewhat less anti-statist than anarchists, and varying in their interpretation of opposition to monopoly, many persons have assumed the label "Libertarian." Intellectual leadership to contemporary libertarians has come primarily from the works and writings of three persons: Ludwig vonMises, F.A. Hayek, and Ayn Rand.

After fleeing Hitler's Germany, vonMises produced his monumental *Human Action*, examining economics, social philosophy, and the scientific method. He concluded that man's true destiny is in free-market activity. F.A. Hayek duplicated this scholarly approach in *Law, Legislation and Liberty*, and other works on classical Austrian economics. In her novel *Atlas Shrugged* and in *Capitalism, the Unknown Ideal*, Ayn Rand claimed that "Property rights are a particular kind of human right, crucially necessary if individuals are to be truly tree."

In the 1970s, the Libertarian movement is visible in a growing number of published articles, journals, books and conferences attended by over a thousand persons.

Somewhat contrary to their principles, they have organized the Libertarian Political Party, which proposes to repeal laws rather than enact more. Their favorite candidates for high office are Roger McBride of Virginia and John Hospers of California. Articulate leaders also include Murray Rothbard of Brooklyn Polytechnic Institute, Thomas Szasz of Syracuse Medical Center, Milton Friedman of the University of Chicago, Karl Hess and Henry Hazlitt.

Ralph Borsodi and the School of Living:

In the 1970s, Ralph Borsodi's works reappeared on many fronts. Wanting Borsodi's *This Ugly Civilization* for his and other students, Dr. Robert Fogarty arranged its republishing by Porcupine Press of Philadelphia. In his introduction, Dr. Fogarty says, "Borsodi is more than a reactive critic intent on duplicating the past; he is a dynamic social philosopher for whom a solution is not 'politics' but scientific domestic production. Borsodi's advice on home economy finds a ready audience from the readers of *Family Circle* as well as *Mother Earth News*.

DECENTRALISM

In December, 1976, Dr. Patrick R. Norris traced the life and message of Ralph Borsodi in 150 pages of his doctoral thesis at the University of Minnesota, *The Post-Industrial Agrarianism of Dr. Ralph Borsodi and Austin Tappan Wright*. Dr. P. Leverette of Furman University of Greenville, North Carolina, planned, in 1977, a doctoral thesis on the intellectual history of 1930 to 1950, and Ralph Borsodi's impact upon it.

In 1975, Doubleday published Scott Burns' 250-page book, *Home, Inc*. With Borsodi's exact method of cost-analysis, Dr. Burns of the Central New England College of Technology showed the overwhelming success of the American household as an economic institution. He proved that even in the high-wage and inflationary 1970s, it still pays to do-it-yourself in everything from making yogurt to painting and refurnishing one's own home. Burns astonished Americans by showing that one could invest in a home with a higher return than in giant corporations.

Burns joined Borsodi in praise of non-monetary (imputed) income:

> When you raise, prepare and serve a Thanksgiving turkey, repair a broken faucet, have friends in for an evening of conversation or charades, you have no more cash in your pocket, but your 'imputed' income has gone up. Such produced at home items are not part of the Gross National Product, but they raise your standard of living and are not subject to taxes. In today's reality of limited resources, more from less is required. But the 'market' is geared to 'more and more'. The household fits an environment where materials and energy are increasingly scarce…A household economy is currently growing faster than the market economy. Non-monetary household income is now almost 50% of disposable cash income. In spite of some invisibility, the household economy may be the only instrument for a positive and livable future.

The School of Living is no longer alone in teaching and promoting modern homesteading. A course is now available in the College of at Davis, California. A School of Homesteading is operated from his homestead by Prof. Maynard Kaufman of the Western Michigan University. Their students learn by field trips to functioning homesteads and rural centers as well as by lectures and doing on a working homestead. A School of Christian Homesteading is located at Oxford, New York. The Rural Life Center of Walthill, Nebraska, fosters small-scale family farming and the modern homestead.

Carla and Mike Emery and their five young children homestead and conduct a School of Country Living at Kendrick, Idaho. Central is Carla's 700-page book on country life, which she wrote, mimeographed (with the help of friends and neighbors) and sold herself. Her difficulties and rebuffs would have discouraged a more timid soul. With hundreds of copies of her book and her five children, she would drive four or five hundred miles to a fair or conference, only to find the meeting postponed. Several times she sold only three or four books. Undaunted, she would find a spot on radio or TV to talk about her homestead, her school, and her book. Eventually she won. From 1974 to 1977, she sold 30,000 copies, averaging $10, and she now has 200 bookstore accounts, a national publisher, a national reputation, and more engagements than she can handle.

Manas magazine, itself decentralist in values and emphasis, summarized the School of Living in Vol 30., March 23, 1977:

> Students in the Twenty-first Century will probably study economics out of E.F. Schumacher…Historians will point out that in the Twentieth Century, the Dark Ages reached bottom, and neither humans nor their planet could stand the way things were going. Social studies may not be needed, considering the changes that will have come about, but there will doubtless be attention to the teaching and examples of Gandhi and Vinoba, and some study of the works of pioneers like Arthur Morgan and Ralph Borsodi.
>
> Borsodi, for example, called for radical change in 1928 with his book, *This Ugly Civilization*, and a year or so later, he published an account of the direction his own life was taking in *Flight From The City*. He described his homestead in Suffern, New York, where he founded the School of Living in 1936.

Awareness of the need for schools of living has grown apace. Today, whether or not their inspiration is traceable to the pioneering of Borsodi and his colleague, Mildred Loomis, there are many similar efforts under way, some of them actual schools on a piece of land somewhere, some centers located in cities where inventive individuals are discovering and teaching ways to transform sterile urban areas into vital neighborhood communities.

Some of the new magazines amount to 'schools of living,' with contents devoted to practical means of creating new ways of self-support and living on the land. For example, *Rain* of December, 1976, tells about a designer and manufacturer whose ingenious and comfortable canvas furniture wins prizes, and who says, 'I feel a void when the basis for my contact with people is money.'

More and more people are refusing to found their lives on the cash nexus. Every person who attempts this freedom is conducting a school for living in his various relationships.

we encounter decentralists

Hundreds of thousands of Americans are decentralists who don't know they are—they have little if any conscious philosophy of decentralism, but if queried, would say they prefer health to disease, voluntary action to governmental control, fair return for their labor rather than economic injustice, small rather than large cities, and country life rather than urban penthouses or tenements.

It would be well if more and more people better understood and could articulate the principles and practices of decentralization. It is the modern version of the early American dream of Liberty. But because of weaknesses and faults in "the American Way," champions of opposite philosophies on the Left and Right make their claims known. American citizens are being enticed into the ideologies and practices of Fascism and governmental types of Socialism and Communism. One reason for this book is to assist both demonstration and articulation of decentralization as a way to both Liberty and Security.

To one who sees the need, range, and implications of decentralism, the current American scene—in spite of a general characteristic of Bigness—is hopeful. Evidence of decentralism appears daily, without even searching for it.

Almost everyone's mail contains this evidence in releases, newsletters, and journals. By 1977, *Mother Earth News* was on the coffee tables of many ordinary middle class and affluent people, as well as in the homes of New Agers. The *Good Earth Catalogue* is the Sears-Roebuck of the decentralist counter-culture. Directories of decentralist New Age groups appear: *Alternative America* carries 5,000 names and addresses of individuals, groups, and publications in that framework. Another in preparation anticipates 10,000 entries—in natural foods and healing, organic agriculture, free-market economics, and anti-statist politics. It is impossible to describe more than a few samples.

Acres USA, Raytown, Missouri, in 1970 became the first newspaper on a national scale devoted to ecological and organic farming. It is primarily news—it talks to, and about, farmers who handle their farms with compost, mulch, green cover, ground rock, avoiding chemicalized sulfurized fertilizers and sprays. In a typical issue, editor Charles Walters explains the mystery of mycorrhiza fungi, shows pictures of corn 18 feet tall grown on seaweed fertilizer, interviews prominent organic farmers, and outlines how eco-farming fares profitwise. Editor Walters tackles decentralization on the economic and political fronts, too. Readers know his aversion to bureaucracy and governmental blunders in items on taxation and on legislation affecting farmers and the energy crisis. Adeptly, Walters challenges that science and technology have gotten out of hand. He is a factor in a true green revolution.

Beginning in 1947, *Manas* magazine has few equals among independent journals for permanence and quality. A weekly, concerned with the "study of principles that move world society on its present course, and with search for contrasting principles," *Manas* is decentralist in orientation. It supports individual action, small communitive, and non-exploitive economics. Ideas of Emerson and Plato flow through its pages with discussions by Dr. Arthur Morgan, John Holt, Ralph Borsodi, Theodore Roszak, and, of course, the ecologists, new alchemists, and doers in "alternative America."

Green Revolution of The School of Living continues in its 37th year as a 40-page bi-monthy, discussing all aspects of living, reporting and synthesizing decentralist thinking and action. A decentralist coalition in 1979 named Mark Satin head of Alliance for a New Age.

A decentralist movement is evidenced and advanced by its own media. But decentralist themes have also reached the public press with articles on all aspects of decentralization. National Public Education television also carries good documentaries on such themes as community improvement, or Dr. John Kenneth Galbraith's "Land And People." Perhaps, some day it will document a history of the decentralist movement.

Decentralist Libraries

Corollary with decentralist journals are outstanding libraries among cooperatives, communes, and individual homesteaders. Typical is the outstanding collection of books on the shelves, available to customer rental and purchase, at the natural food restaurant, Yes!, bordering Washington, D.C., in Arlington, Virginia.

Matching in variety and importance is the Lefever library at Sonnewald Homestead in Spring Grove, Pennsylvania., which carries nearly a thousand books. Here are all the challenges to health mentioned in this book, emphasizing that "food is one's best medicine." Books are shelved by subject: health and herbs, sprouting seeds, composting, organic gardening, country living, longevity, ecology, conception, child-birth and breast feeding. There are scores of books on natural therapies for cancer, heart disease, muscular dystrophy and arthritis, on high and low blood sugar, on vegetarian and macrobiotic cooking, yoga, biofeedback, fluoridation of water, and the politics of health.

The Colemans in Maine and the Kerns in California are other well-known homesteaders whose libraries and published booklists add to the service they render. One can get an excellent annotated bibliography on biological agriculture from Eliot Coleman, founder of the Small Farm Research Association, Harborside, Maine. As associates of Scott and Helen Nearing, the Colemans include most of the seminal books written during the 1930s and 1940s. Faber and Faber of London are the noted publishers of many of these significant books, while Devin Adair in Old Greenwich, Connecticut, and Rodale Press of Emmaus, Pennsylvania, have grown to become leading publishers of organic agriculture in the U.S.

Ken Kern Enterprises, Oakhurst, California, publishes the *Owner-Built Homestead*. Kern culls his recommendations in his current catalog down to 15 on home-building and 12 on homesteading. He lists six titles on Alternative Technology, and six more on Diet and Health.

DECENTRALISM

Revolt In Education

A growing number of decentralists follow John Stuart Mill in his conclusion:

> A general state education is a contrivance for moulding people to be exactly like one another; the mould in which it casts them is that which pleases the predominant power in the government.

Questions of arbitrary authority in public school education is rampant. Everywhere school and college faculty are responding to (and sometimes initiating) restless activity of students. "What is education for?" is widely discussed in professional journals. Students, and professors too, are dropping out of colleges; thousands of parents find ways to educate their children outside the public school system. Experimental, free and "open" schools (children from four to twelve years of age in one room) are common. Schools which advocate freedom with responsibility—following philosophies of Maria Montessori, Rudolph Steiner, Alfred Adler—increase.

Paul Goodman's *Compulsory Mis-Education* (1970) and *Community of Scholars* outlined new concepts and approaches. Albert Jay Nock raised questions of government in education in *Theory of Education in the U.S.* Ivan Illich wrote *Deschooling Society*, and John Holt writes *Why Children Fail* and *Instead of Schools*. Holt maintains that children (and adults) learn from actual experience, not from contrived or pretended activity. Instead of school, children need access to the real world, in their homes and communities. In *A Primer of Libertarian Education*, Joel Spring said that reform in education results only from restructuring society without authoritarianism, and examines the relevancy of theories for change of Godwin, Ferrer, Illich, Stirner, Marx and others.

A surge has developed of persons seeking education on their own. They travel at home and abroad, crisscrossing the USA to visit, communicate, and work with persons living alternate lifestyles on homesteads, in communes, in cooperatives, or with those who are writing, thinking and working out challenging ideas. The Lefever Homestead and other School of Living Centers constantly receive such visitors for a few hours, or days, or months. They appear singly, in small groups, sometimes in busloads.

They ask eager questions about whole foods, self-sufficient living, community development, education, religion, radical economics, and anti-statism. Thousands of new-age counterculture groups have similar visitations.

Uncounted conferences and conventions are organized on all aspects of living. Interchange and intercommunication take place on all manner of decentralist concerns—anything from natural childbirth to population control; from bee-keeping to solar energy; from homesteading to world peace; from "victims of cancer" to the major problems of society. Thousands of people attend craft and community fairs in all seasons. Exhibits include "appropriate technology" in building, furnishing, heating, lighting, plumbing, such as the Swedish Clivus Multrum waterless self-composting indoor toilet.

On a recent auto trip from the East to Mid-America, we quite unexpectedly encountered decentralists at almost every stop. One evening, we stopped in New Lebanon, Ohio, with a couple old enough to have retired to their rocking chairs. Instead, they are active homesteaders. They served us a cool, green drink of comfrey and edible weeds blended in apple juice. (The green drink was made famous by Dr. N.W. Walker, now 103 years old, who with a young wife is parent to three children, the youngest 21 months.) A delightful supper of their own fresh steamed vegetables and raw salad was followed by inspection of their garden, lush with rows of twelve different vegetables, herbs, and flowers. The next day, we visited our hostess' father, over 90 years old—he too was in his garden, collecting greens for his daily potion. Hale and hearty, he maintains his home and is president of the local natural food club. Hundreds of motorists pass by his garden, unmindful of this meaningful aspect of a decentralist movement—a healthy, aged man, satisfied with his lot, and in no need of help other than from his family.

At nearby Lane's End Homestead, our friends, John and Joanna Peterson, Antioch college grads, keep to Lane's End self-maintenance farming, including weaving on our cherry loom. Because of it, they were invited to demonstrate it on a Bicentennial Farm on cross-country Interstate 70. To thousands of visitors they said, "We are not only 'exhibiting' diversified, do-it-yourself homesteading, but it is our chosen way of life."

We drove through Ohio, Indiana, to Champlain, Illinois, where we enjoyed the hospitality of a professor of biology at the University. We were prepared for the correct suburban area they lived in, and for their comfortable split-level house. What surprised us in this setting was the active health-food store in their garage. For some thirty friends, they bought whole grains, rice, honey, molasses, dried and fresh fruit, juices, nuts, oils. Through pooled orders and once-a-month pick-up, they did a business sometimes amounting to $8,000 a month.

At Madison, Wisconsin, we visited Bruce Allison and friends working out a Community Land Trust to take land in southeastern Wisconsin off the speculative market.

Returning, we looked up a local dentist in Wheeling while our car was repaired. We found him teaching patients and supplying them with literature on *Applied Nutrition—A Preventative of Dental Caries.*

Later, we stopped for gas. We got acquainted with a busload of young people from California, awaiting another car in their caravan. They told us they were part of a "Fellowship of the Magic Circuit," and as a declaration of their faith in love and goodwill as the way to world peace, they were en route to Washington to urge U.S. President Carter to ban all nuclear projects. When we asked them how, in a world of unearned wealth, they would rid the world of poverty, they said, "The Community Land Trust is part of the solution!" Here was a completely chance meeting with wayfarers bringing our cherished reform to the front.

While this has been a report of decentralism mainly in the land of Jefferson, USA, we remind ourselves that the struggle between Liberty and Authority is universal and world-wide. The desire for freedom is basic among maturing human beings; yet the impulse to power and control over others often takes precedence in immature humans. In 1980, movements for liberty and participation are finding various decentralist expressions in every section of the globe.

In India, of course, it continues with the Gandhians, including the Janata Party and Vinoba Bhave. In England, the late E.F. Schumacher, presented his *Small is Beautiful*, now used world-wide. In Switzerland the small, local cantons continue; in the Netherlands and Scandinavia decentralists are active; in Italy decentralists rally around Danillo Dolci; in France Lanzo del Vasta and The Arc communities; in Mexico Ivan Illich leads with *Tools of Conviviality*. In many South American and African countries non-statist groups work for a voluntary society. Is it too much to hope that, as human maturing increases, all these will federate into a world alliance for liberty?

26
summary and challenge

A fourth American Revolution is in process—a Decentralist Revolution firmly rooted in the basic, freedom-loving, decision-making nature of human beings. Persons, ideas, and activities are included in these pages because they use and fulfill those essential human aspects. In at least four ways, these activities provide what earlier American political, racial, and industrial revolutions neglected or failed to supply.

1. Decentralist life-ways are in harmony with Nature. The "discovery" of North America was a heady business, giving the colonizers reason for thinking that Man had assumed command, and was thus fulfilling God's will. Rather than to live in harmony with the beautiful land they found as did the other residents of North America, they assumed that the great expanse of the continent had been preserved especially for them to develop, manage, and exploit. The colonists had to work out the relationship of one human being to another, and wrote that in the U.S. Constitution. But no where in the original papers of the United States of America is there reference to the relationship of human beings to land and nature.

Americans concentrated on exploration and exploitation. Promptly, science and technology produced tools that made war seem inevitable. Giant machines, factories, and cities were not only goals, but became realities. In the 1960s and 1970s, for the first time in 200 years, the participants in Western Civilization had to seriously think about their place in nature. Modern homesteaders, whose lives by choice have been based on the land, are presented for evaluation.

2. Individuals and groups are included in *A History of the American Revolution* who are aware of two grave errors—in the possession of the earth and in issuing money with which to exchange goods. Again, no principle or counsel in those crucial matters are in the nation's original documents. The U.S. Constitution guarantees the right to life, liberty, and the pursuit of happiness, but no guarantee to land. In his *Agrarian Justice*, Thomas Paine championed this right to be included. "Not the earth itself, only the improvements on it can be treated as property to be bought and sold," Paine declared. Yet legalized private property in land became an ingrained American custom, with its long train of speculation, mal-distribution of wealth, poverty and conflict. School of Living decentralists countered this age-long error with Community Land Trusts, recognizing land as the heritage of all, granting rights to occupy to those who use it.

Similarly, while the Constitution gives the U.S. Government the right "to coin money," in reality, money is controlled and directed by private banks, mistakenly called a "Federal system." Government retains the right to print and issue money for wars, for payment of national debt, and other non-productive use. The resulting unlimited inflation robs workers, consumers, and the savers of money, through continuous rises in prices. Decentralists offer non-inflationary currency in cooperative, voluntary, local associations.

3. The units of organization in a fourth, post-industrial revolution are small. Decentralists heed Ralph Borsodi's recommendations to keep units of production, ownership, control, education, government, and population small enough to allow persons involved to meet face-to-face, to know the facts, to really understand and deal with the issues at hand.

4. When cultural affairs are operating on the above three principles—in harmony with nature, removing land and money monopoly, and people-control in small local groups—*then* voluntary action replaces coercion, and then "the State will wither away." When land is free or available at low cost, when money is stable and credit inexpensive, each individual in a free market will receive what he has earned, none will have what he did not produce, and all persons can follow their inclination for a lifeway. As an invitation and challenge to a creative, human life-style, we have de-

scribed homesteads and homesteading, people using natural instead of drug-healing, people implementing appropriate technology, and cooperative, voluntary associations, and carrying on education for living suited to both children and adults. Decentralists are making progress in their essential American, fourth Revolution. Any daily newspaper tells why decentralism is so necessary.

Although Americans live longer, have more wealth and education than at any time during the century, America ranks first in the world in murder; violent crime against people and property tripled in the last 15 years. The annual rate of divorce and annulment has more than doubled. Although Americans spend more time in school, the practical knowledge of educated persons has declined. Less than half can complete income-tax and insurance forms without help.

With more free time, fewer work-days, and lowered age-retirement, three out of ten say their favorite pastime is watching television; 30 million watch major league baseball, and horse racing draws twice as many fans. This adds up to something less than an Age of the Quality-Minded. Yet even in this milieu, decentralists are confident. With William James, they

> ...are done with big things, big institutions, and big success. They are for those small, invisible, moral forces which, like the oozing of water, if given time, will rend the hardest monuments of man's pride.

To those who claim "there is not enough time left" to allow non-violent, persuasive forces to win, the answer comes: "in employing decentralist forces we create stability and extend our time." The choices are clear and increasingly persons are choosing decentralist alternatives.

> *Each worthy cause for a future glorious*
> *By quietly growing becomes victorious,*
> *A cause can neither be lost nor stayed*
> *Which takes the course of what Truth has made,*
> *And is not trusting in walls and towers*
> *But slowly grows from seeds to flowers.*

índex

167

community and money
men and women making change
Mary-Beth Raddon

At the beginning of the 21st century, the three most important concerns in the developed nations are remarkably convergent— unemployment, the environment, and community breakdown. Because we will have to live with these issues for the foreseeable future, only a long-term structural approach can successfully resolve these problems. This book examines how community currencies could contribute to tackling all three problems.

Through a combination of theory, practical implementation, and personal interviews, Mary-Beth Raddon offers a guide to some very attractive alternatives to traditional currency transactions.

> A highly recommended book for those working towards alternatives to the global economy. —Susan Witt, Executive Director, E. F. Schumacher Society, Massachusettes

> Extensive interview material is used to draw out key ideas in a way that combines depth of analysis with accessibility.
> —Mary Mellor, *Feminism and Ecology* and *The Politics of Money*

> One of those rare books that succeed on a number of levels...it is the drama of idealistic individuals moving against the tide of the mainstream economy to revitalize their communities through the use of local currencies or trading networks.
> —Jeffrey Jacob, *New Pioneers: The Back-to-the-Land Movement and the Search for a Sustainable Future*

MARY-BETH RADDON, teaches at Brock University in St. Catharines, Ontario. She holds a Ph.D. in Sociology from the University of Toronto.

216 pages, 6x9, bibliography, index
Paperback ISBN: 1-55164-214-X $19.99
Hardcover ISBN: 1-55164-215-8 $48.99

participatory democracy
prospects for democratizing democracy

Dimitrios Roussopoulos, C.George Benello, editors

A completely revised edition of the classic and widely consulted 1970 version

First published as a testament to the legacy of the concept made popular by the New Left of the 1960s, and with the perspective of the intervening decades, this wide-ranging collection probes the historical roots of participatory democracy in our political culture, analyzes its application to the problems of modern society, and explores the possible forms it might take on every level of society from the work place, to the community, to the nation at large. Part II, "The Politics of Participatory Democracy," covers Porto Alegre, Montreal, the new Urban ecology, and direct democracy.

> The book is, by all odds, the most encompassing one so far in revealing the practical actual subversions that the New Left wishes to visit upon us.—*Washington Post*

Apart from the editors, contributors include: George Woodcock, Murray Bookchin, Don Calhoun, Stewart Perry, Rosabeth Moss Kanter, James Gillespie, Gerry Hunnius, John McEwan, Arthur Chickering, Christian Bay, Martin Oppenheimer, Colin Ward, Sergio Baierle, Anne Latendresse, Bartha Rodin, and C.L.R. James.

DIMITRIOS ROUSSOPOULOS is a political economist who has written extensively on social issues. He is the author of many books including *The Public Place* and *Dissidence: Essays Against the Mainstream*.

C.GEORGE BENELLO (1927-1987) taught sociology at Goddard College in Vermont until his untimely death. He was also a Fellow of the Cambridge Institute and author of *From the Ground Up: Essays on Grassroots and Workplace Democracy*.

380 pages
Paperback ISBN: 1-55164-224-7 $24.99
Hardcover ISBN: 1-55164-225-5 $53.99

ALSO AVAILABLE from

Bakunin: The Philosophy o f Freedom, Brian Morris
Bringing the Economy Home from the Market, Ross V.G. Dobson
Canada and Radical Social Change, Dimitrios Roussopoulos, editor
Coffee With Pleasure, Laure Waridel
Commonwealth of Life, Peter Brown
Decentralizing Power, Taylor Stoehr
Designing Utopia, Michael Lang
Dissidence: Essays Against the Mainstream, Dimitrios Roussopoulos
Humanity, Society and Commitment, Kenneth McRobbie, editor
Myth of the Market, Jeremy Seabrook
Perspectives on Power, Noam Chomsky
Politics of Social Ecology, Janet Biehl, Murray Bookchin
The Public Place, Dimitrios I. Roussopoulos
Toward a Humanist Political Economy, Phillip Hansen, Harold Chorney
Water Crisis, Julie Stauffer

send for a free catalogue of all our titles
BLACK ROSE BOOKS
C.P. 1258, Succ. Place du Parc
Montréal, Québec
H2X 4A7 Canada

or visit our web site at: http://www.web.net/blackrosebooks

To order books:
In Canada: (phone) 1-800-565-9523 (fax) 1-800-221-9985
email: utpbooks@utpress.utoronto.ca
In United States: (phone) 1-800-283-3572 (fax) 1-651-917-6406
In UK & Europe: (phone) London 44 (0)20 8986-4854
(fax) 44 (0)20 8533-5821
email: order@centralbooks.com

Printed by the workers of
MARC VEILLEUX IMPRIMEUR INC.
Boucherville, Québec
for Black Rose Books Ltd.